Flutter App Development Made Easy: A Step-by-Step Guide

Honor .G Zavala

All rights reserved. Copyright © 2023 Honor .G Zavala

__Funny helpful tips:__

Practice appreciation; regularly express gratitude for each other.

In the realm of possibilities, cultivate a mindset that sees opportunities, not just obstacles.

Flutter App Development Made Easy: A Step-by-Step Guide : Effortlessly Learn Flutter App Development with Expert Tips and Strategies: Your Ultimate Learning Companion.

<u>Life advices:</u>

Invest in employee well-being; a motivated team boosts productivity.

Stay informed; knowledge empowers and enlightens.

Introduction

This is an informative guide that delves into the world of cross-platform development using Flutter. Designed to cater to individuals who are new to Flutter and seeking to acquire comprehensive knowledge about its functionalities, the guide provides an in-depth exploration of the fundamental concepts and practical techniques essential for building Flutter applications.

The guide commences with an introductory overview of Flutter, emphasizing its significance in cross-platform development and highlighting the reasons for learning it. It discusses the anatomy of a Flutter app and presents an analysis of the pros and cons associated with learning Flutter, allowing readers to gain a well-rounded understanding of its capabilities and limitations.

Readers are then introduced to the setup and installation process, along with the technical requirements necessary for building apps with Flutter. The guide proceeds to outline the step-by-step process of creating a Flutter app from scratch, encompassing topics such as working with assets, loading images, and adding app icons for iOS and Android projects. It also delves into the intricacies of deploying Flutter apps to physical devices, offering comprehensive guidance and troubleshooting tips to facilitate a seamless deployment process.

Furthermore, the guide explores the various Flutter widgets and their functionalities, enabling readers to build beautiful user interfaces efficiently. It delves into the usage of container widgets, column, and row widgets for layout creation, offering insights into real-world examples and best practices for incorporating these elements into Flutter applications.

As the guide progresses, it delves into the implementation of custom fonts, material icons, Flutter cards, list tiles, and the integration of state management within Flutter applications. It provides comprehensive instructions and guidelines for leveraging gesture and user input functionalities, encouraging readers to experiment with different features and gain a comprehensive understanding of their capabilities.

Overall, this book serves as a valuable resource for individuals seeking to embark on their journey into the world of Flutter development, offering comprehensive insights, practical techniques, and hands-on experience to facilitate the development of efficient and visually appealing Flutter applications.

Contents

Chapter One: Introduction To Cross-PlatformDevelopment with Flutter 1
   1.1   What is Flutter? 1
   1.2   Why Learn Flutter? 3
   ●   It's pretty easy to get started with and develop. 3
   ●   Flutter has well-organized documentation and a robustcommunity. 3
   ●   It offers quick compilation with the attendant maximumproductivity 4
   ●   You can use Flutter to create startup MVPs 4
   The Anatomy of the Flutter App 5
   1.3   Pros and Cons of Learning Flutter 6
   ●   Quicker app development 7
   ●   Easier to Maintain and Develop New Features 7
   ●   A Perfect Choice for Advanced UI 7
   ●   Easy to Adapt to Different Screen Dimensions 8
   ●   Access to Device Features 8
   ●   Simultaneous App Updates on Android and iOS 8
   The Cons 8
   ●   Fewer numbers of Flutter developers 9
   ●   Platform Limitations 9
   Chapter Summary 9
Chapter Two: Set Up and Installations 11
   2.1   Requirements for Building Apps with Flutter 11
   2.2   Overview of App Building Process 12
   Core principles 12

2.3   Windows Installation Steps – Installation of Flutter SDK, Android studio, and Android emulator. 15
1.   Install the Flutter SDK 16
2.   Install Android studio 17
3.   Set up your Android device 18
4.   Install the Flutter and Dart plugins 18
2.4   Windows Installation and Troubleshooting 18
2.5   Mac Installation Steps - Install the Flutter SDK, Androidstudio, Android emulator, and Xcode 19
2.6   Test the iOS Simulator on Mac 20
Create and run a simple Flutter app 22
2.7   Mac Installation Troubleshooting 22
Fix: 23
2.8   Configure Android Studio for Flutter Development 25
Technical Requirements 28
Chapter 2 Tip – Get your act together! 28
Chapter Three: Let Us Create a Flutter App fromScratch 30
3.1   Creating A New Flutter Project From Scratch 30
Create and run a simple Flutter app 30
3.2   Scaffolding A Material App 32
Properties of Scaffold Class: 33
3.3   Working With Assets in Flutter and the Pubspec File 35
Specifying Assets 35
Accessing Assets in the Flutter App 35
Loading Images 37
Output: 37
Loading images from package dependency: 38

Loading Assets: 40
3.4   How to Add App Icons to the iOS and Android Projects 40
iOS Icons 41
Android Icons 41
Chapter Four: Running Your App on a PhysicalDevice 44
4.1   Deploying Flutter Apps to a Physical Device 44
Developer options. 45
4.2   How to Deploy Flutter Apps to Physical Android Devices 45
1.   Configure your Android device 46
2.   Configure your computer 46
OS X 46
3.   Establish a local connection 47
4.   Set up a connection over wifi 47
4.3   How to Deploy Flutter Apps to Iphone/IpadDevices 48
Troubleshooting: 50
Deploy the same app to another iOS device 51
Deploy a new app 51
Chapter Summary 52
Chapter Five: How to Build Beautiful UIs withFlutter Widgets 54
5.1   A One Screen Personal Business Card App - Micard 54
5.2   The Flutter Power Tools - Hot Reload and Hot Restart 55
Real World Example 55
How to perform hot reload in your app 57
5.3   How to Use Container Widgets 57
Constructor of the container 60
this.child: 61
Color color: 61

this.padding:	62
Width and height:	64
this.margin:	64
this.alignment:	66
constraints:	70
tight	71
loose	71
expand	71
decoration and foregroundDecoration	73
ShapeDecoration	75
BoxDecoration	76
this.transform	78
5.4 How You Can Use Column and Row Widgets for Layout	80
5.5 Flutter Layout Challenge	102
Layout of the App	104
● Navigation Bar	104
● Welcome Text	105
● Buttons	107
● Service Request	109
● Middle and Bottom Sections Container	111
● Bottom Container	112
Create the SquareButton Widget	117
The Page Review	120
PageView.	128
The Drawer	129
How to create the drawer layout	130

Animate the Drawer	132
Creating the Shadow	136
The menu items list	137
User Information	140
5.6 Tapping into the Widget Properties	146
5.7 Incorporating Custom Fonts in Your Flutter App	152
5.8 Adding Material Icons With the Icon Widget	156
5.9 Flutter Card and ListTile Widget	159
Properties of ListTile Widget	160
Chapter Summary	165
Chapter Six: Building Apps with State	165
6.1 A stateful dice app (Dice Project)	166
6.2 Using the Expanded Widget for Flexible Layouts	171
6.3 How to Use Intention Actions	175
How to use intention actions in Flutter	176
6.4 Dart Functions Part	178
Function Parameters	178
How to use parameters	178
The void main() function	179
6.5 Dart Variables	181
Rules for Creating a Variable in dart	181
How to Declare Variables	182
Annotations in Dart	182
How to Declare Multiple Variables	183
Assigning of a Variable in Dart	183
Declaring Default Value	183
Using Final and Const	184

6.6	Dart Data Types	185
Chapter Seven: Deploying Gesture and User Input		188
7.1	Stateful Versus Stateless Widgets	188
7.2	Detecting User Interaction With Flutter Buttons	191
	Chapter Summary	210
Chapter Eight: Dice Image Challenges		211
8.1	Making the Dice Image Change Reactively	211
8.2	Randomizing the Dice and Challenge One	214
8.3	Challenge One Solution and Challenge Two	219
8.4	Challenge Two Solution And Challenge Three	222
8.5	Challenge Three Solution	223
Final Words		226

Chapter One: Introduction To Cross-Platform Development with Flutter

Developing a mobile application is such a tedious job, but there are several frameworks available to create a mobile application. Android offers a native framework powered by Java, while iOS provides a native framework based on Objective-C or Swift language. Both frameworks are great choices when developing Native applications specifically for their respective devices.

However, to create an application that supports both operating systems, we need to write programs in two different languages using two different frameworks. To help deal with this difficulty, there are mobile frameworks that support both operating systems.

These frameworks can be hybrid mobile application frameworks that use HTML for User Interface (UI) and JavaScript for application logic. Also, the frameworks could be a complex language-specific framework that performs the heavy job of converting code to native code.

This is where the concept of Flutter comes to play. Regardless of how simple or complex these frameworks might be, they always have some drawbacks and one of the major disadvantages is that they perform very slowly.

In recent years, mobile applications have continued to become more popular. As a result, many coding tools are now available to developers who want to create programs. Among these tools, there is Flutter, whose popularity is increasing.

1.1   What is Flutter?

Flutter is an open-source, cross-platform toolkit that helps developers build native interfaces for both Android and iOS. Flutter is a free and open-source mobile UI framework created by Google and launched in May 2017. Simply put, it allows you to create a native mobile application with only one codebase. This means that you can use one programming language and one codebase to create two different apps (for iOS and Android).

Flutter consists of two important parts:

- **An SDK (Software Development Kit):** A collection of tools that are going to help you develop your applications. This includes tools to compile your code into native machine code (code for iOS and Android).
- **A Framework (UI Library based on widgets):** A collection of reusable UI elements such as buttons, text inputs, sliders, and so on that you can personalize for your own needs.

Dart, a programming language, is required to write code with Flutter. The language was created by Google in October 2011, but it has improved a lot over the last few years. It's an open-source and object-oriented programming language. Dart applies to both client- and server-side development.

This programming language is more concerned with front-end development. Thus, you can use it to develop mobile and web applications. If you're experienced with programming, Dart is a typed object programming language. You can compare Dart's syntax to JavaScript. Dart has a lot in common with Kotlin, Java, C#, and Swift. If a developer knows some of these languages, it won't be hard for them to switch to Flutter.

Flutter uses Dart, and its user interface layout requires no extra templating languages such as XML or JSX, or any special visual tools. This allows programmers to create a structural platform and interactive widgets and reuse them. Flutter has an architecture that includes widgets that feel and look good. They are fast, customizable, and extensible.

Many controls, libraries with animations as well as other customizable tools increase native UI development, including widgets.

Because of all of the above, programmers don't need to switch to a design mode thinking about what to do. In Dart coding, everything is available in one place. The idea is to reuse code, and Flutter does that well for standard app cases.

1.2   Why Learn Flutter?

Developers actively use Flutter, and Google plays a large part in that. For example, Google's AdWords platform was built with the help of Flutter. This brings to the question: why should you learn Flutter?

That said, let's see why Flutter should be the app development language you choose:

- **It's pretty easy to get started with and develop.**

Flutter is easy to learn and use. First, setting up Flutter on a Windows, Mac, or Linux machine is a simple process and Google has even bundled Dart with the Flutter installation package so all components are installed at once.

Flutter uses 'widgets' which makes the UI easy to use. All features that you would need to build an app are provided as building blocks, or widgets. This gives developers complete control over app development while making the process of development easy.

- **Flutter has well-organized documentation and a robust community.**

Google continually invests in improving Flutter and Dart. They recently released the Fuchsia programming language policy which stated Dart is one of the primary languages to build apps for future OS. This clearly shows the language is increasing in popularity.

Flutter is also ranked second on GitHub's 2019 *fastest-growing open-source projects by contributors* list.

The increased popularity and use of Flutter have created an active and helpful support community. There are online documentation, support forums, and libraries like:

- *Flutter Awesome:* A website that curates Flutter libraries and tools.
- *Awesome Flutter:* A GitHub repository for Flutter support.
- *It's all widgets!:* A repository of different apps built with Flutter.

There are Flutter events that bring the community together, helping developers grow and solve problems.

- **It offers quick compilation with the attendant maximum productivity**

Thanks to Flutter, you can change your code and see the results in real-time. It's called Hot-Reload. It takes a short amount of time when you save to update the application itself. Some changes force you to reload the app. However, if you perform a task such as design, for instance, the change in the size of an element happens in real-time!

- **You can use Flutter to create startup MVPs**

If you want to show your product to investors as soon as possible, you can use Flutter!

Minimal Viable Product (MVP), is a minimal version of the final app. It is usually built to run beta tests through focus groups and to pitch the product to investors. MVPs are an important part of the app development process today. The whole idea of building an MVP revolves around speed and efficiency: building a product with the essential features quickly.

Companies today prefer to work with development tools that can deliver good results fast. Flutter is quickly gaining ground as it greatly enhances the power of the MVP development process. Flutter is ideal to build MVPs because of the following reason:

- The code works on both Android and iOS, eliminating the need for multiple apps and devices.
- The performance of an app built on Flutter is on par with a native application.
- The development process is easy because of the use of widgets which reduces build time.
- The ease of use also reduces the number of resources needed both man and machine.
- It is supported by both Android studio and visual studio code.

An IDE, or Integrated Development Environment, is a software that provides the tools needed for application development. Tools such as a source code editor, debugger, compiler, interpreter, etc. are integrated onto a single program, the IDE, to simplify the process of software development.

Flutter is available on different IDEs. There are different IDEs available today that developers can choose from depending on preference and programming language. The advantage of learning Flutter is that it has extensions for different IDEs, such as Android Studio and Visual Studio (VS) Code, the two most popular code editors.

Developers have the freedom to select the IDE they are most comfortable using when programming with Flutter because Flutter and Dart have plugins that support these IDEs.

The Anatomy of the Flutter App

Now, to understand the anatomy of the Flutter app better, we must know what the widget tree is all about. So, let us get started with the explanation of a widget-tree. It is the structure of the Flutter app, covering scaffolding and planning an app by using simple blocks before the actual programming and it will solve many of your design problems in advance.

The first thing to do is to create a Scaffold. The scaffold is nothing but a blank screen in purple color. Inside the Scaffold, there is an AppBar at the top of the screen (in red).

Below that, we have a Container (in blue) which is just a whole box; inside the Container, there is a Column (in yellow), which is a column-like structure that will contain widgets.

Within the Column, there is a Row (in green); here we are stacking the widgets inside the Column vertically, hence, in this case, it is called a Row.

Now, you might be wondering where to add or call it a Column and where to add or call it a Row, So, here is a simple distinction: if the Widgets are aligned side by side horizontally, they are Row Widgets and if they are aligned one below the other vertically then they are a Column.

Below that, there is a piece of Text. Now, the widget tree is complete as respective to the Image of the Device. There can still exist multiple nested widgets (widgets inside widgets). For example, you can add two widgets side by side horizontally inside the Row that may be two pieces of different texts, or an image (using Image Widget) and text, or an image and an icon (using Icon Widget).

You see, for everything you want to do in your App, there is a pre-defined Widget for that. You can customize these Widgets according to your choice.

1.3   Pros and Cons of Learning Flutter

Flutter is a promising cross-platform solution that has its advantages and disadvantages. Flutter can be used for building many apps. However, it cannot cover all platforms, like browsers, launchers, or apps that depend heavily on platform API.

Here are the advantages of using Flutter:

- **Quicker app development**

Flutter is a cross-platform solution, so one codebase can be run on both Android and iOS. This saves a lot of development time. Of course, it will not be cut in half, but it is safe to emphasize that writing one codebase for both platforms will take less time than writing separate projects for both platforms.

- **Easier to Maintain and Develop New Features**

When your apps are ready and published, you can focus on expanding your user base. Oftentimes, this translates to moving the app into maintenance, where fixing errors is a major concern and adding new features becomes a secondary issue.

- **A Perfect Choice for Advanced UI**

Flutter renders all parts of the interface using an internal graphics engine called Skia. This is the same engine that is used in Google Chrome and Mozilla Firefox. Skia is a quick and well-optimized software that allows Flutter to work differently than many other mobile development frameworks.

Using Flutter is more like writing a game. From the operating system, you get a blank canvas, and all UI elements are drawn by application. The Flutter team put great work to recreate material UI components and Apple Design System elements internally.

Moreover, you can also make your own components; this is where Flutter will shine. It is easy to develop good looking custom UI elements. In addition to that, you will have these elements work on both Android and iOS. This makes Flutter a perfect choice for apps with advanced, customized UI designs.

- **Easy to Adapt to Different Screen Dimensions**

Flutter's layout system makes writing and fitting views to various screen sizes easier than iOS SDK. This makes the creation of animations smoother than in native iOS and Android. Moreover, looking at the roadmap of Flutter, we shouldn't wait long for support for desktop and web applications.

- **Access to Device Features**

One of the main reasons why people are afraid of cross-platform solutions is access to native features. After all, what makes your app stand out on a simple webpage is the use of camera, GPS, or haptic feedback. You can use these features in Flutter as well.

- **Simultaneous App Updates on Android and iOS**

The same codebase for both platforms allows you to release app updates at the same time. This task is difficult to execute, especially when there are different projects for the two platforms. Also, longer implementation on one platform makes synchronizing difficult. The problem increases when an application update requires changes in the backend service.

Flutter and other cross-platform tools eliminate this problem because we make applications for both platforms at the same time. It is important to note that the iOS application must pass Apple review every time it is updated.

The Cons

- **Young Technology**

With every new technology comes a risk that it will evolve in a way we don't want to follow, or maybe (God forbid!) it will be dimmed by its creator. The fact that Flutter is sponsored and developed by

Google and it plans to use it in its new OS makes this scenario unlikely. Nevertheless, it is good to know about this.

- **Fewer numbers of Flutter developers**

The other thing is, there are fewer Flutter developers on the market than native iOS and Android ones. Personally, though, I would not worry about this point, because experience shows us that mobile developers are willing to learn Flutter, and learning it turns out to be a quite enjoyable experience.

- **Platform Limitations**

Flutter's own UI rendering nature adds some limitations. For instance, if some features are incorporated into the UI on native platforms, they should be recreated by the Flutter team. There are two examples that we already identified: video player and iOS profile data completion.

However, the truth is that, in native development, we usually cannot add new system features from release day because we have to keep system compatibility.

Chapter 1 Tip – The earlier, the better...

Flutter has a ton of potential and is easy to get started with. If you're a programmer who just wants to make coding faster, more efficient, and compatible, Flutter is just for you. Start coding now!

Chapter Summary

We took ample time to study the basics of coding with Flutter. By now, you should be familiar with the meaning of Flutter, the reasons why Flutter is spreading like wildfire, the pros, and cons, and many more.

In the next chapter, you will get to know how to prepare your environment for Flutter development. You will understand the following concepts:

- Flutter with Android studio
- Dart plugins
- Everything about set up and installation

So, come along as we explore the Flutter ecosystem!

Chapter Two: Set Up and Installations

In this chapter, we'll discuss in detail about how to set up Flutter, knowing full well that the concept of Flutter is the latest buzz in the app development market. Flutter has become a widespread framework in recent times. Let's learn how to install and use Flutter for the benefit of our business.

2.1 Requirements for Building Apps with Flutter

You need two pieces of software to complete this program. They are the Flutter SDK and an editor.

You can run the program by using any of the following devices:

- An Android or iOS device linked to your computer. It must be set to developer mode.
- The iOS simulator (requires installing Xcode tools)
- The Android Emulator. This requires setup in Android Studio.
- A browser (Chrome is required for debugging)

If you want to compile your app to run on the web, you must enable web support which is currently in the testing stage. To enable it, use the following instructions:

$ Flutter channel beta

$ Flutter upgrade

$ Flutter config -enable-web

You need only run the config command once. After activating web support, each Flutter app you develop also compiles for the web. In your IDE under the **devices** pulldown, or at the command line using Flutter devices, you should see **Chrome** and **Web server** listed. The **Chrome** device automatically starts Chrome. The **Web server** begins a server that houses the app so that you can load it from any browser. Make use of the **Chrome** device when creating apps so that you can use development tools. Also, use the webserver when you want to test on other browsers.

2.2 Overview of App Building Process

The essence of having an overview of the app building process is to enable developers to deliver high-performance apps that feel natural on different platforms. We welcome differences in certain areas such as typography, scrolling behaviors, icons, and others.

This is a demonstration app from the Flutter gallery (running app and repo). It is a collection of Flutter sample apps. Shrine has high-quality scrolling images, interactive cards, buttons, dropdown lists, and a shopping cart page.

No mobile development experience is required to get started. Apps are written in Dart, which is similar to Java or JavaScript. Experience with object-oriented languages is definitely helpful, but even non-programmers have made Flutter apps in the past!

Core principles

Flutter consists of the most recent react-style framework, a 2D rendering engine, ready-made widgets, and development tools. These components work in agreement for the purpose of helping you to design, build, test, and even debug apps. Everything is organized around a few core principles.

Everything's a widget

Widgets are the fundamental building blocks of a Flutter app's user interface. Every widget is an unchangeable expression of part of the user interface. In contrast to other frameworks that separate views, see controllers, layouts, and other properties, Flutter is composed of a stable and unified object model called the widget.

A widget can define:

- a structural element (such as a button or menu)

- a stylistic element (such as a font or color scheme)
- an aspect of the layout (such as padding)
- and many more

Widgets form a hierarchy based on composition. Each widget sets within and inherits properties from its parent. There is no separate application object. Instead, the root widget serves this role.

You can respond to events, such as user interaction, by telling the framework to replace a widget in the hierarchy with another widget. Then, the framework checks the similarities and differences between the new and old widgets. It efficiently updates the user interface.

Composition

Widgets are made up of a variety of small, single-purpose small devices that join forces together to produce powerful effects. For instance, the Container is a commonly-used widget that is composed of many widgets. These widgets control layout, painting, positioning, and sizing. Specifically, Container is made up of Padding, LimitedBox, DecoratedBox, ConstrainedBox, Align, and Transform widgets. So, instead of classifying Container to produce a personalized effect, you can arrange these, and other simple widgets in new ways.

The classification is both shallow and broad to increase the possible number of combinations.

You can also control the layout of a widget by composing it with other widgets. For instance, to place a widget at the center, you enclose it in a Center widget. There are widgets meant for grids, padding, row, alignment, and columns.

These layout widgets have no individual visual representation. Rather, their personal aim is to control some areas of another widget's layout. Oftentimes, it is beneficial to check the neighboring widgets to know why a widget renders in a certain way.

Layer cakes are delicious

The Flutter framework is arranged in a set of layers, with every layer building upon the former layer. The upper layers of the framework are used more frequently than the lower layers.

Also, the goal of this design is to help you do more with less code. For instance, the material layer is developed by arranging basic widgets from the widgets layer. Then, the widgets layer is built by arranging lower-level objects from the rendering layer.

The layers provide a lot of options for developing apps. You're required to select a personalized approach to open the complete expressive power of the framework. You can even use building blocks from the widgets layer, or mix and match. On the other hand, you can arrange the ready-made widgets Flutter provides. Or better still, you can create your custom widgets by using the same tools and techniques that the Flutter team used to build the framework.

Nothing is hidden from you. You have many productivity benefits to reap. They include a high-level and unified widget idea and others.

Building widgets

You define the unique characteristics of a widget by implementing a *build()* function that returns a tree (or hierarchy) of widgets. This tree represents the widget's part of the user interface in more concrete terms. For instance, a toolbar widget could have a build function that brings back a horizontal layout of some text and many different buttons. The framework then asks every widget to develop until the process phases out in complete concrete widgets. The framework then joins together into a tree.

A widget's build function should have no side effects. But, any time it is asked to build, the widget should bring back a new tree of widgets no matter what the widget returned in the past. The framework does the heavy lifting of comparing the previous build with the current build and determining what modifications need to be made to the user interface.

This automated comparison produces good results thereby activating high-performance and interactive apps. The design of the build function simplifies your code by focusing on declaring what a widget is made of, rather than the complexities of updating the user interface from one state to another.

If the special features of a widget need to change based on user interaction or any other factors, that widget is *stateful*. For example, if a widget has a counter that increments whenever the user taps a button, the value of the counter is the state for that widget. When that value changes, the widget needs to be rebuilt to update the UI.

These widgets are classified below Stateful Widget instead of Stateless Widget and store their changeable state below State. Whenever you change a State object (for example, by incrementing the counter), you must call *setState()* to signal the framework to update the user interface by calling the State's build method again.

Having separate state and widget objects lets other widgets treat stateless and stateful widgets in the same way, without being concerned about losing state. Rather than needing to hold on to a child to preserve its state, the parent is free to create a new instance of the child without losing the child's persistent state. The framework does all the work of finding and reusing existing state objects when appropriate.

Now that you're familiar with the basic structure and principles of the Flutter framework, along with how to build apps and make them interactive, you're ready to start developing and iterating.

2.3 Windows Installation Steps – Installation of Flutter SDK, Android studio, and Android emulator.

The system requirements for installing Flutter on windows are as follow:

For you to install Flutter on your windows PC, your development environment must have the following minimum requirements:

Operating System: Windows 7 SP1 or later (64-bit)

Disk Space: 400 Mb (Except disk space of IDE/tools)

The tools for Flutter installation depend on these tools being available in your environment, Windows PowerShell, Git for Windows.

1. Install the Flutter SDK

Step 1- Head over to URL https://Flutter.dev/docs/get-started/install/windows and download the most updated Flutter SDK.

Step 2- Open the zip file and add the contained Flutter in the installation location for the Flutter SDK. For instance, **C:/src/Flutter**. You may not install Flutter in a directory such as **C:/Program Files/,** as it requires some relevant privileges.

Step 3- Update your path

Go to the Start search bar, type 'env' and *select "Edit environment variables for your account".*

Look for an entry called Path which is located under the user variable *che*.

Under Path click on the new tab and type the complete path to *Flutter/bin*. Your full path should look like *C:/src/Flutter/bin*.

Step 4 - Flutter has a tool called Flutter doctor which checks your environment to ensure that all the requirements of Flutter development are met.

Flutter Doctor

Step 5 – When you run the above command in Flutter environment, it will analyze your system and give a report such as the one shown below:

"Doctor summary (to see all details, run Flutter doctor -v):

[√] Flutter (Channel stable, v1.2.1, on Microsoft Windows [Version 10.0.17134.706], locale en-US)

[√] Android toolchain - develop for Android devices (Android SDK version

28.0.3)

[√] Android Studio (version 3.2)

[√] VS Code, 64-bit edition (version 1.29.1)

[!] Connected device

! No devices available

! Doctor found issues in 1 category."

The above report shows that all development tools needed are available but no device is connected. So, this issue can be fixed by connecting a physical Android device through USB to your computer or starting an Android emulator.

2. Install Android studio

Download and install Android Studio from this link, https://developer.Android.com/studio

Open the file to run the Android Studio. It's simple to run, just launch the *"Android Studio Setup Wizard"*. It'll install the most up-to-date version of Android SDK and other tools required by Flutter for

Android development. Other tools include the Android SDK Platform and Android SDK Build Tools.

3. Set up your Android device

To run and test your Flutter app on an Android device, you'll need a physical Android device running Android 4.1 or API level 16 and above.

1. Enable **Developer Options** and **USB debugging** on your device.

2. Windows-only: Install the Google USB Driver.

3. Using a USB cable, plug your phone into your computer. If it requests that you authorize your computer to access your device, go ahead and authorize it.

In the computer, run the command of Flutter devices to ensure that Flutter recognizes your connected Android device. Flutter makes use of the version of the Android SDK where your *adb tool* is based by default. So, if you want Flutter to use another installation of the Android SDK, you'll have to set the *Android_home* environment variable to that installation directory.

4. Install the Flutter and Dart plugins

Open Android Studio.
Click Configure > Plugins.
Select the Fluter plugin and click install.
Also, click yes to install the Dart plugin.
Restart Android Studio.

2.4 Windows Installation and Troubleshooting

Congratulations! You have installed Flutter on your desktop. Just to ensure that everything you did is running and working fine, search for 'command prompt'. A black window should appear. Type in —

Flutter — version

Hopefully, you'll see something similar to this.

If you don't see the above message, try retracing the above steps and be extra careful with the Path variable and .zip file extraction.

Again, if after running Flutter doctor, it does nothing after checking the Flutter version but gets stuck and doesn't check for Android toolchain or anything else you may not have proper the Java installation, and fixing your Java will fix your Flutter and make it run without problems.

If your Flutter installation fails, it seems you have not pasted the **PATH** in the Environment Variables Account. You have to take Flutter (Extracted folder), and paste the path up to *Flutter/bin* in the Edit Path table. Then, try running Flutter doctor from the folder in a computer where you have your Flutter folder.

2.5 Mac Installation Steps - Install the Flutter SDK, Android studio, Android emulator, and Xcode

You'll need a Mac operating system in addition to other requirements mentioned at the beginning of this chapter for the installation of Flutter on Mac.

To set up Flutter on Mac operating system, you will have to take the following steps:

Step 1 – Grab your mouse and point your cursor to this URL, https://Flutter.dev/docs/get-started/install/macos. Download the latest Flutter SDK.

Step 2 – Open the zip archive in a folder, say /path/to/Flutter

Step 3 – Update the system path with Flutter bin directory (in ~/.bashrc file).

> *export PATH = "$PATH:/path/to/Flutter/bin"*

Step 4 – Use the command below to activate the updated path in the current session and verify it as well.

source ~/.bashrc

source $HOME/.bash_profile

echo $PATH

Step 5 – Install the most recent copy of XCode, if it is requested by Flutter doctor

Step 6 – Also, install the latest Android SDK based on Flutter doctor's report.

Step 7 – Run latest Android Studio, if reported by Flutter doctor

Step 8 – Open an Android emulator or connect a physical Android device to the computer to build an Android application.

Step 9 – Start iOS simulator or connect a physical iPhone device to the computer as well to create iOS applications.

Step 10 – Install these two important tools for Android Studio, they are Flutter and Dart plugin. They provide the startup system to develop a new Flutter application. It does not stop there, they also offer the option to install and debug Flutter applications in the Android studio itself and many more options.

Follow the steps below to install both tools.

- Open Android Studio
- Click **Preferences** → **Plugins**
- Select the Flutter plugin and click Install
- Click yes when requested to install the Dart plugin.
- · Restart Android studio.

2.6 Test the iOS Simulator on Mac

Apple and Google offer excellent developer tools such as the real simulators and emulators of the mobile devices with powerful configuration possibilities. In this section, I'm going to describe step-by-step how to install and configure iOS simulators as well as test your Flutter app on iOS simulator.

Pre-requirements

You need a Mac to test your website in iOS Simulator since iOS developer tools are only available on the Mac operating system. This is a major requirement. Android developer tools are cross-platform as such you can install them on Mac, Windows, and Linux.

Install iOS Simulator

iOS Simulator is a part of Xcode, which you've already installed on your system. If you've not done so, you can download and install it for free from the App Store's link https://itunes.apple.com/by/app/xcode/icl497799835?mt=12 using your Apple developer account.

It downloads around 5.5 GB, so the installation takes longer, depending on your network connection.

When you're done installing the Xcode, open it from the Launchpad. Then, accept the license or agreement and wait for some ancillary installations. If you see the Xcode welcome window, know that your installation is successful.

Since you're not an iOS app developer, you don't need to create any projects there. As a web developer, all you need is to run the iOS simulator. Open *Xcode* in the menu bar, *click developer tool* followed by *Simulator*.

Adding more versions and devices in iOS Simulator

You have the option of changing either the version of iOS or the device hardware which is running it. Open the *Device* menu item under *Hardware* in the menu bar. There is a list of currently available operating systems.

If you want additional versions of simulated iOS, go back to Xcode and choose preferences in the *Xcode* menu bar item. Head over to the components tab to view a list of every available iOS version. There's a tiny arrow down icon close to the simulator name, click on it to download your desired version. The simulator images are usually big. Therefore, the file will take some time to download.

Create and run a simple Flutter app

Here are the steps to follow to develop your first Flutter app and test the setup:

Develop a new Flutter app by executing the following commands:

$ Flutter create my_app

This creates the *my_app* directory which contains Flutter's starter app.

CD into this directory:

$ cd my_app

To run the app in the Simulator, make sure that the Simulator is running. Then, type the command below and hit the enter key:

$ Flutter run

2.7 Mac Installation Troubleshooting

If you're having some issues installing the Mac operating system, you may diagnose the problem by checking through the installation log. When you do, you can restart the installation of Mac OS once again. However, if you want to boot up your computer using another disk, then select Startup Disk from the utility menu.

The error message has four options: Shut Down, Restart, Save Log, and View Log. It is highly likely that restarting your computer will produce the same error message.

Updating your Mac is usually a very simple process. However, in some cases, you may encounter errors like this one. Please note that it has been reported that this issue may occur even when no upgrade or update is initiated. If your Mac freezes in the middle of a Mac OS update and it did not boot up, here is how you can fix it:

Note that before trying anything, you should ensure you back up your device.

Fix:

The first thing you should try is to start your Mac in safe mode. You can do so easily: Simply restart your computer and as soon as your computer begins restarting, press and hold the Shift key, until you see the Apple logo. This will put your computer into safe mode. Try to update or upgrade your Mac now. If this does not work, read on.

The next thing you should try is to start up your Mac using Startup Manager. Here is how:

1. Turn off your Mac

2. Turn on your Mac

3. Immediately after turning on your Mac, press and hold the Option (alt) key

4. You will see the Startup Manager popup, now you can release the Option key

5. Select your regular/standard (usually Macintosh HD) disk and click the arrow icon under it and hit Enter.

If you are still having this issue, try repairing your disk. Here is how:

1. Restart your Mac, and while your computer restarts, immediately press and hold the Command and R keys until you see the Apple logo, then you can release the keys.

2. macOS Utilities will launch

3. Select Disk Utility and click Continue

4. Run First Aid.

5. If First Aid says the Disk is OK, then, on your computer, go to System Preferences> Users & Groups> and click the Login Items tab, if you see any third-party apps there, click the minus icon and remove them. And try again.

If nothing above helps, follow the steps below:

1. Depending on the macOS version you are trying to install, try using the macOS combo update. These update files are available on Apple websites. They are big files so it will take time to download and install.

2. Locate the macOS combo update from Apple's support center at https://support.apple.com/downloads/macos and Click Download

3. Once the download is completed, double click to run and to see if this completes the installation.

If you are still having problems try this.

1. Power off your Mac.

2. Power on your Mac and immediately press and hold Command (⌘)-R

3. You will see the macOS utility window

Select *"Reinstall macOS"*, this option will install the most recent version of macOS on your Mac. Click *Continue* and follow the onscreen instructions.

2.8 Configure Android Studio for Flutter Development

We will start with Windows installation steps first for those who use Windows Machines. *Bear in mind that you will only get Android output when using the Windows machine because a Mac machine with Xcode is needed for iOS development.*

1. Download and install Android studio from https://developer.Android.com/studio/index.html.

2. Install **Git for Windows** from this link https://git-scm.com/download/win with the *Use Git from the Windows Command Prompt option* enabled during installation

3. Open Command Prompt by either writing cmd in *Run window or* by using *Start Menu* like Start=> Windows System => Command Prompt (in Windows 10)

4. Get Flutter SDK: Write and execute the following code in a terminal window,

   git clone -b beta https://github.com/Flutter/Flutter.git

5. After running the above command, Flutter will be downloaded in the folder where you have executed the command. For you to execute Flutter commands, we need to set up the PATH environment variable for the current user by following these steps.

6. Head over to the Control Panel. From the dropdown menu, click on User Accounts and select "Change my environment variables".
7. Under "User variables" check if there is an entry called "Path", In most cases, it's there, so select it and click edit to open the below-given Window and edit it or else click on New to create this variable and give the path of Flutter or bin folder
8. Restart Windows to fully apply this change
9. Now open *Command prompt* again and execute the Futter doctor command which will check your environment and display a report to the terminal window. Also, it will show the errors; in any case, it'll ask you to install Android SDK and Android Studio (as you missed installing it earlier):
10. Keep on executing the commands mentioned in the result of Flutter doctor until you get the following message which says that Flutter installation is all ok:
11. Now Open Android Studio. On the welcome screen click on *Configure => Plugins*:
12. On the Next screen click on *Browse* button
13. Now on the browse screen, search for Flutter by typing the same in the Search Bar and click Install button.
14. This will ask to install Dart also, as Flutter is dependent on Dart. Select Yes for that dialog and install both.
15. Immediately the Plugin installation is completed, it will require you to restart *Android Studio. When you're done* restarting the plugin, then the message "*Start a new Flutter Project"* will appear on the welcome screen.
16. Congratulations - Flutter with Android Studio is installed in your machine.

Configuring Android studio on Mac OS:
1. Install Xcode 12 or newer through the **Mac App Store**.
2. Download and install **Android Studio**.
3. Open Terminal window either by using programs or searching for it.

4. Get Flutter SDK: Write and execute the following code in a terminal window:

    git clone -b beta https://github.com/Flutter/Flutter.git
5. Once the above step is complete, execute the following command to add the Flutter tool. Set local user path variable for the time being, for the current computer window:

    export PATH=`pwd`/Flutter/bin:$PATH
6. Execute *$PATH* command again which will show the list of all paths mentioned in $PATH variable and the path of your Flutter installation will be added to it.
7. Now, run Flutter doctor command as it will check your environment and show a report to the computer window. Also, it will show the errors in bold. In this case, it'll ask you to upgrade Flutter and install Brew.
8. Keep on running the commands reported in the result of Flutter doctor. Remember that all installations are done through the command prompt. The steps to include Flutter plugin in Android Studio and developing new Flutter projects are exactly the same as in Windows.
9. After completing the project creation wizard, the IDE screen with default code will be the same as Windows. The toolbar will show the devices connected to your system or emulator together with the run button. However, if you click on the drop-down arrow of the devices option,

you will have the chance to start the iOS emulator as well as other Android emulators.

Technical Requirements

In your bid to learn to code in Flutter, you will need these tools:

- A PC with a recent Windows version, or a Mac with a recent version of the macOS or Linux operating system. You can also use a Chrome OS machine, with a few tweaks. Currently, the only way to build apps that target iOS devices is by using a Mac, unless you use a third-party service. Of course, you can write your code on any operating system, but the .ipa file, which is the iOS installation file, can only be created from a Mac.
- A GitHub account.
- An Android/iOS setup. You'll need to set up your Android and iOS environments to build apps.
- The Flutter SDK. It's free, light, and open source.
- Physical device/emulator/simulator. In order to try your code, you will need an Android or iOS device. Alternatively, you can also install an Android emulator or iOS simulator.
- Your favorite editor. The supported editors at this time are:
- Android Studio/IntelliJ IDEA
- Visual Studio Code

Chapter 2 Tip – Get your act together!

A journey of a thousand miles begins with a mile. To learn coding with Flutter, you need to prepare your system which is what this chapter has dwelt on. Having prepared your system with all the necessary installations and configuration, it's time to move forward.

Chapter Summary

- This chapter dealt more with how to install Flutter and set up the environment required for Flutter app development. It didn't stop there, it went further to investigate the requirements for building apps with Flutter.
- Other points discussed included windows installation steps, windows installation, and troubleshooting, Mac installation steps as well as troubleshooting issues, plus how to test the iOS simulator on Mac.
- Moving forward, we'll get into the much interesting aspect of coding with Flutter, which is to create a Flutter app from scratch in the next chapter.

Chapter Three: Let Us Create a Flutter App from Scratch

In this chapter, we are going to learn how to create a simple Flutter application from scratch and to understand the basics of the Flutter application.

3.1 Creating A New Flutter Project From Scratch

Now that everything is set up, we're ready to create the first Flutter project from scratch. The first option is to create a new project on the command line by using the Flutter command. But before that, let's create and run the first simple app in Dart command line.

Create and run a simple Flutter app

Develop a new Flutter app by executing the following commands:

$ Flutter create my_Flutter_app

This creates the *my_Flutter_app* directory which contains Flutter's starter app. By using the option **create,** you're telling Flutter to create a new project. The name of the new project folder is specified by using the second parameter. After the project is created you can change into the newly created project folder:

CD into this directory:

$ cd my_Flutter_app

In this directory, you can start the default Flutter application in the simulator by using **the Flutter command with option run**. So, make sure that the Simulator is running. Then, type the command below and hit the enter key:

$ Flutter run

You'll see the output on your computer or any device you're using to run it which is shown on the command line after the app has been launched successfully.

Now you should be able to see the result in the simulator. The default Flutter app is a very simple one. It consists of four elements:

- AppBar on top which contains the text *Flutter Demo Home Page*
- Two text element in the center position
- An action button

If you click on the plus (+) button at the right bottom, the counter which is displayed in the middle of the screen is increased by one.

You can also perform all the steps directly in the Visual Studio Code. Do you know why? It is because we've installed the Flutter extension before you can find various Flutter commands when opening up Visual Studio Code command palette by using shortcut ⇧⌘ P and typing in *Flutter* to search for all Flutter-related commands.

Here you can find commands such as to create a new Flutter project *Flutter: New Project*, launch the emulator with *Flutter: Launch Emulator*, or select the SDK location with *Flutter: Change SDK*.

Once the project is created and the emulator is started you can start the Flutter project in debug mode by using the *Start Debugging (F5)* menu entry or just hitting F5 on your keyboard.

The project is then launched in the already running emulator and inside Visual Studio Code, you'll see another control bar that can be used to control the execution of the app.

On the other hand, you can create a new project for Flutter by working with Android studio. All you have to do is to start the Android studio, go to File, click New, and new Flutter project. There are three Flutter applications to choose from: Flutter application, Flutter plugin, and Flutter package.

- Choose **application** if you want to develop the app for end-users.
- Choose **plugin** when you're exposing an Android or iOS API for developers.
- Lastly, you can choose **package** when you're creating a pure Dart component, such as a new widget.

Now it's time to create a new project. On the welcome screen, choose **Start a new Flutter Project** and select **Flutter Application** on the next screen.

The next step is to select a name for your project and enter a path to your SDK. If SDK is not specified, just click on "Install SDK."

Choose the package name and add support for Swift and Kotlin (if necessary). Finally, set your domain name for the package. It's important for package names to be unique (for signing and publishing purposes). If you don't own a domain, use com.github.<your login> . Leave the other options set to default values and confirm by clicking Finish.

After clicking the Finish button, it will take some time to create a project. When the project is ready, you will get a fully working Flutter application with minimal functionality.

Basically, that's all you need to start working on a project.

Additionally, you can run a default code generated with Flutter (don't forget to run an emulator or connect your device).

3.2 Scaffolding A Material App

Scaffold is a class in **Flutter** which provides many widgets or APIs such as Drawer, SnackBar, BottomNavigationBar, FloatingActionButton, AppBar, etc. It expands or occupies the whole device screen or the available space. The scaffold provides a framework to implement the basic material design layout of the application.

The Scaffold widget is a framework that includes the standard screen components.

Properties of Scaffold Class:

AppBar - AppBar is used to display the toolbar and other widgets at the top of an application. AppBar is placed at the top of the application. It has its own properties such as elevation, title, brightness, etc.

Body - The body is the primary content of the Scaffold. It will display the main or primary content in the Scaffold. It is below the *appBar* and under the *floatingActionButton*. The widgets inside the body are at left-corner by default.

Floating Action Button - Floating Action Button is an icon button which majorly resides at the bottom left corner of the screen. It is called so because of its nature, it hovers over the data and performs actions when clicked.

Drawer - Drawer is a slider menu or a panel that is displayed at the side of the scaffold. The user has to swipe left to right or right to left according to the action defined to access the drawer menu. In the *Appbar*, an appropriate icon for the drawer is set automatically at a particular position.

The gesture to open the drawer is also set automatically. It is handled by the Scaffold. Alternatively, the drawer is a panel hidden on mobile devices and shown when a button is pressed or on right/left swipe of the screen. The drawer has **ListView** as its component part while the drawer **header** and **ListTile** are the components of **Listview**.

Bottom Navigation Bar - Bottom Navigation Bar is a scaffold widget used to display a navigation bar at the bottom. This bar is made up of many items such as an icon, text or both of them. We use *BottomNavigationBar* widget to display the bar. We can use the *fixedColor* feature to display the color of an active icon.

To include items in the bar, we use *BottomNavigationBarItems* widget. The widget is used to give both text and icon. For the action performed on the tapping on the items, we have *onTap* function which works according to the index position of the item.

Background color – This is used to add color to the background of an application or to set the color of the whole scaffold widget.

Floating Action Button Animator – We use this feature to provide animation to move *floatingActionButton*.

Primary – We use the primary feature to tell whether the scaffold will be displayed or not.

Drawer Scrim Color – It is used to define the color for the primary content while a drawer is open.

Persistent Footer Buttons – This is a list of buttons that are displayed at the bottom of the scaffold. These buttons are visible for a long time, even when the body of the scaffold moves. They will be covered in a *ButtonBar*. Also, they're rendered above the *bottomNavigationBar* but below the body.

End Drawer - An *end drawer* is like a drawer property but in the end drawer, by default, the drawer is displayed at the right side of the screen.

Resize To Avoid Bottom Inset - This property helps both the body and the scaffold's hovering widgets to size themselves. They do this to avoid the onscreen keyboard whose height is influenced by the bottom property.

3.3 Working With Assets in Flutter and the Pubspec File

Flutter applications can comprise both code and assets. An asset is a file that is tied to and used together with your app. It is accessible at runtime. Common types of assets include static data such as JSON files, configuration files, icons, and images of various file formats.

Specifying Assets

Flutter makes use of the *pubspec.yaml* file. The file is located at the base of your project and it works to identify assets required by an app. This is a prerequisite and you will need to specify your assets in your *pubspec.yaml* file like following and then the assets that you mentioned will be bundled with your app and will be available at runtime. Here is an example:

Flutter:

  assets:

     - assets/my_icon.png

     - assets/background.png

To add every asset under a directory, designate the directory name with the / symbol at the end:

Flutter:

  assets:

     - directory/

     - directory/subdirectory/

Remember that only files located directly in the directory are included. To include files located in subdirectories, you'll need to create an entry for each directory.

Accessing Assets in the Flutter App

Loading JSON file:

Create a *config.json* file at path *assets/json/config.json*, and add some JSON as follows:

{

"key1":"value1"

}

Now in your *pubspec.yaml* file specify this file like:

assets:

   - assets/json/config.json

import:

import 'package:Flutter/services.dart';

Create a method to load asset using *rootBundle*:

Future<String> loadAsset() async {

   return await rootBundle.loadString('assets/json/config.json');

}

Working with JSON file in code:

void main() {

  loadAsset().then((value) {

          Map map = json.decode(value);

          map['key2'] = 'value2';

          print(map);

  });

}

Running your app will give the following output:

{key1: value1, key2: value2}

So we have successfully loaded the JSON file and then we parsed that JSON and modified it and printed it in our logs. This should give you enough confidence to work with json files.

Did you have fun working with JSON files? Maybe loading images will provide you more fun. So, let's go!

Loading Images

Loading images is almost similar to loading the JSON file, so what's the difference?

Clone this repository so that you can have the code to follow along.

Notice that in assets/images folder we have folders like 1.0x, 2.0x, 3.0x, 4.0x 5.0x and there are images in them with the same name i.e 'image'. Now, if you try to run this app on devices with different dimensions, you will see that images from different folders are accessed for devices with different dimensions.

This is how Flutter handles the image resolution for devices with different screen sizes.

Output:

On devices with a device pixel ratio of 1.8, the asset .../2.0x/image.png would be chosen. In the same vein, a device having a pixel ratio of 2.7, the asset .../3.0x/image.png should be ideal.

If the width and height of the rendered image are not specified on the *Image* widget, the small resolution is used to scale the asset so that it will occupy equal screen space with a higher resolution just as the main asset would do. That is, if .../image.png is 72px by 72px, then .../3.0x/image.png should be 216px by 216px; but they both will render into 72px by 72px (in logical pixels) if width and height are not specified.

Loading images from package dependency:

Flutter supports the idea of using common packages contributed by other programmers to the Flutter and Dart ecosystems. This makes it easier for them to quickly build an app without having to start from scratch to develop everything.

If you need to load images from an external package, you have a big job to do! This requires that you communicate that package to the *AssetImage* widget. After that, you can use it to access images from that package.

To understand this, we will use *shrine_images* dart package as our image resource and will learn how to use images from packages.

However, to import and use *shrine_imagess* your *pubspec.yaml* should look like this:

name: Flutter_assets

description: A Flutter app.

version: 1.0.0+1

environment:

　sdk: ">=2.1.0 <3.0.0"

dependencies:

　Flutter:

　　　　sdk: Flutter

　shrine_images: ^1.1.2

dev_dependencies:

　Flutter_test:

sdk: Flutter

Flutter:

  uses-material-design: true

  assets:

    - packages/shrine_images/10-0.jpg

Notice two things:

1.   I included *shrine_images: ^1.1.2* as a dependency.

2.   I included — *packages/shrine_images/10–0.jpg* under the Flutter assets. You start with *package/*. Then you give the package name (shrine_images in this case). Then you give the location and file name in the **lib/** folder. You don't include *lib* itself because that is assumed. I am only using one image in my simple app. If I were using more images I would have to list them all individually (like the Shrine app does). You can't just specify the folder like you can with local assets.

Now using above mentioned images in your app your *main.dart* file should look like this:

import 'package:Flutter/material.dart';

void main() => runApp(MyApp());

class MyApp extends StatelessWidget {

  @override

  Widget build(BuildContext context) {

    return MaterialApp(

      home: Scaffold(

        appBar: AppBar(title: Text('My App')),

```
        body: Center(
        child: Image(
         image: AssetImage(
                '10-0.jpg',
                package: 'shrine_images',
           ),
           ),
           ),
           ),
               );
    }
}
```

Note that there is no need to import the *shrine_images* package at the top of the file.

To get the image, you use *AssetImage* and provide it the asset name and package name. *AssetImage('10-0.jpg', package: 'shrine_images')*.

Loading Assets:

Each Flutter app has a *rootBundle* object for easy access to the main asset bundle. *rootBundle* is *The AssetBundle* from which this application was loaded. To load any asset with *rootBundle* you will need to import *package:Flutter/services.dart*.

3.4 How to Add App Icons to the iOS and Android Projects

Application Icons are the unique identification of the App. They're the main thing that the user always remembers. In most cases, the user remembers the application icon instead of the application name. App Icon can be your brand logo or anything else but should define the purpose of your application. If you're tasked with adding app icons on your iOS and Android projects, here's how.

iOS Icons

We're not going to waste time here. All you have to do is to go ahead and download Icon Set Creator at itunes.apple.com/us/app/icon-set-creator/id939343785?mt=12.

Run the software and open it. Drag a 1024x1024 version of your icon onto the application and hit Go (the default platform is iOS so you should be good to go here). Icon Set Creator will give you a folder with all of the necessary icon sizes.

Now that you have all of your icons, open up your project in Xcode. In the main project folder, you'll find a folder called Images.xcassets and a file called AppIcon.

Here you'll see placeholders for icons in your app. If you want to add iPad or CarPlay icons you can hit the button on the top right corner, Show the Attributes Inspector, to reveal more options.

Open up your newly generated icon folder and start dragging and dropping on the appropriate tiles. If it has a 2x or 3x under the tile, use that version. For example, the top-left tile (iPhone Notification iOS 7–11 20pt 2x) will use the file called icon-20@2x.png. Just match up the pt value with the proper scale and you should be all set. Note that iPads use the 1x and 2x versions, while the iPhone uses 2x and 3x versions.

In your text editor you should notice some new files at ios>*ProjectName*>Images.xcassets>AppIcon.appiconset. Should be able to rebuild your app and see your icons (in iOs only)

Android Icons

Hop on over to Android Asset Studio to make all of your Android Icons.

Drag the same icon file you used for the iOS icons (1024x1024) and edit away. Some cool tools here, go ahead and edit your icon so it looks good in all Android icon versions, and hit the Download button in the upper right-hand corner.

Once you have your icon folder, open up Android>app>src>main>res. You should see a bunch of folders in here called mipmap-hdpi, mipmap-mdpi, etc.

The folder you downloaded from Android Asset Studio will have those same folders. Just replace those files and you'll be all set for Android icons.

Chapter 3 Tip - How to ace this course

You've just gone through the basic steps to get you started in building on Flutter from scratch. Flutter is developed based on the understanding of well known mobile apps around where we can easily build user interface components in just a few lines of code. We can see that the global community is investing a lot in this framework, and we could possibly foresee a bright future ahead for Flutter, striving past React Native.

Chapter 3 is a complete guide to the Flutter SDK and Flutter Framework for building native iOS and Android app. It teaches how to run your first Flutter project from scratch.

Chapter Three Summary

- The aim of this chapter is to create a Flutter app from scratch and get started. Fortunately, that's exactly what we've managed to achieve.

- Next, we'll dive straight into running your app on a physical device. It's going to be a lot of fun, as we'll look at how to deploy Flutter apps to iPhone and iPad devices.

Chapter Four: Running Your App on a Physical Device

When you're developing an Android application, it's essential that you always verify or test your App on a real device, including emulators. This chapter describes how to prepare your development environment. It also provides detailed information on how to set up an Android-powered device for both testing and debugging on the device.

4.1 Deploying Flutter Apps to a Physical Device

In chapter three, you created your first simple Android app. It is time to run the app on a physical device or an emulator.

The following steps should guide you to set up your device and run the app on a physical/real device.

1. Plug your device to your development machine using a USB cable. If your development environment is on Windows, you will likely need to install the right USB driver for your device.

2. You need to enable **USB debugging** in the **Developer options** window. Here are the steps:

a) Open the **Settings** app.

b) If your device uses Android version 8.0 or higher, select **System**. If not, proceed to the next step.

c) Move your cursor down to the bottom and click **About phone**.

d) Scroll to the bottom and tap **Build number** seven times in quick succession.

e) Return to the previous screen, scroll to the bottom, and tap **Developer options**.

f) In the **Developer options** window, scroll down to find and enable **USB debugging**.

Did you find these steps easy? Now, let's proceed to run the app on your device as follows:

1. Open the Android studio and select your application from the run/debug configurations drop-down menu in the toolbar.

2. Open the toolbar and select the device that you want to run your application on from the target device drop-down menu.

   a. Click Run.

   b. Android Studio installs your app on your connected device and starts it. You now see the app running on your device.

4.2 How to Deploy Flutter Apps to Physical Android Devices

Multiple Android phones and tablets can be plugged to a computer via a USB cable. However, the connection between an Android device and a computer via a USB connection is limited to file transfer only.

So, if you want to use your device to develop an Android application, you will need to apply some configuration changes to your device as well as your computer. In this section, I'll show you how to make those changes.

To follow along, the major requirements you should have are:

- The latest version of the Android SDK
- An Android device with an Android OS of 4.2 or above

So, how can we go about it? Here we go:

1. Configure your Android device

Since the majority of Android users are not app developers on devices running Android 4.2 or higher, all the settings meant for app developers are hidden by default. You need to unhide all these settings. How? Click on the **settings** on your device and navigate to **About phone**. Then, locate the Build **number** and click on it seven times in quick succession.

When you do this, you should be able to see the **Developer options** menu. Open it and make sure that the **USB debugging** option is checked.

In addition, it would be helpful if you check the **Strict mode enabled** and **Show CPU usage** options as well. Enabling these options will make it easier for you to tell if you've gone out of the right coding practices.

Now that you're done with all these configurations, your device is ready to be used for app development. Just connect it to your computer via its USB cable.

2. Configure your computer

The configurations, settings, and other changes you need to make on your computer are based on the operating system it has. Here, we focus on OS X and Windows.

OS X

On OS X, you don't have to make any changes at all.

Windows
If you're using Windows 7 or higher, you have to download and install an **Original Equipment Manufacturer** USB driver for your

Android device. Just go to the website of the device manufacturer and download the driver. But, if you are using any of the Google Nexus iOS products, installing the Google USB Driver is compulsory.

3. Establish a local connection

Having properly configured both your Android device and your computer, it is time to start the Android Debug Bridge server. What it does is to automatically establish a connection between them.

Navigate to the **platform-tools** directory of the Android SDK and use the following command to start ADB.

adb start-server

Once the server is ready, a dialog will display on your device's screen requesting you to confirm if you want to permit USB debugging. Also, the dialog holds certain essential data such as the RSA key fingerprint of your computer. Press **OK** to establish the USB connection.

Henceforth, you can use your device to create apps rather than the Android emulator. If you are using Android studio, on pressing the **Run** button in the toolbar, you will see your device in the list of running devices.

4. Set up a connection over wifi

Many Android programmers and developers use multiple Android phones and tablets to check how their apps look and behave on various screen sizes including Android versions. Connecting all these devices to a computer via USB cables can be difficult. So, ADB helps in this regard by allowing developers to connect to their devices through a Wi-Fi network.

To prepare your device for debugging through a Wi-Fi connection requires that you connect it to your computer using a USB cable. In addition, ensure that both the computer and the device are connected to the same Wi-Fi network. You must open a port on the device on which it can listen to TCP/IP connections using the command below. For instance, this is how you can open port **5565**. Just type this:

adb tcpip 5565

Next, you need to determine the IP address of the device. Go to the app's **settings** on the device, locate the **About phone** feature and click on **Status**. You are able to see its IP address, in both the IPv4 and IPv6 formats, under the **IP address** heading.

Now that you know both its IP address and port number, you can disconnect your device from your computer, and connect to it over Wi-Fi using the following command. For instance, if your device's IP address is 192.168.0.4, this is how you would connect to it:

adb connect 192.168.0.4:5565

From this point on, you can use the device for Android app development just as you would use one connected over USB.

4.3 How to Deploy Flutter Apps to Iphone/Ipad Devices

Deploying Flutter apps on an iOS device like iPhone or iPad is not cumbersome. It rather requires you to have the following two major components:

1. An Apple account – Open the App Store on your device (Mac), click sign in, then click create new Apple ID. You can also go to www.support.apple.com for additional help on creating an apple account on your device.

2. Homebrew installed - Homebrew is package manager for Macs which makes installing many different software such as Git, Ruby, and Node simpler. Homebrew helps you to avoid possible security issues associated with using the *sudo* command to install software such as Node.

As a matter of fact, you should be familiar with the Mac Terminal application as you'll need to use it to install Homebrew. Beside that, you can find the terminal application in the utilities folder of the applications folder.

The installation requires that you open the terminal app and type the following command:

ruby -e "$(curl -fsSL https://raw.githubusercontent.com/Homebrew/install/master/install)"

You'll see direction in the terminal explaining what you have to do to finish the installation process.

The next step is to set up physical device deployment in Xcode. The process is equally straightforward. Run the following commands in your terminal:

$ brew update

$ brew install — HEAD libimobiledevice

$ brew install ideviceinstaller ios-deploy cocoapods

$ pod setup

$ cd <YOUR FLUTTER PROJECT DIRECTORY>

$ open ios/Runner.xcworkspace

1. The last line should open the default Xcode workspace. In that workspace, choose the *Runner* project which is located in the left navigation panel.

2. In the *Runner* target settings page, ensure your Development Team is selected under **General > Signing > Team**. After selecting a team, Xcode develops as well as downloads a Development Certificate as usual. It also registers your device with your account, and creates and downloads a provisioning profile if required.

One of the conditions that must be met before you commence your first iOS development project is that you must sign into Xcode using your Apple ID. To get everything straight, you also need to ensure that *Bundle Identifier* is a unique string.

Then go into the "Signing & Capabilities" tab (may be called "Signing" depending on your version of Xcode), and select your team.

Now you're ready to run *Flutter run* in the terminal! Your app is on your device!

Troubleshooting:

If you ran into any issues with brew, run **brew doctor** in your terminal and follow those instructions to resolve the issue.

When you connect your device with a USB cable, a dialogue may pop up that asks you to "Trust this computer". Click "Trust". However, if the dialogue does not pop up, you will have to set it manually by navigating to settings on your device.

If you run into issues, "Start your app by running 'Flutter run'.", (i.e. "bash: run: command not found"). You can simply click the *Run* button or play icon in Xcode.

A dialogue may pop up on your computer requesting for a password. If it persists to pop up even after you have entered your user password (the password you use to sign into your computer account), click "Always Allow" instead of "Allow". Many of these windows will pop up, so ensure you fill out all of them. Then Xcode should finish running your app.

When Xcode is done running your app, the app icon should appear on your device. If you haven't "trusted" the computer on your device, a dialogue will appear that says "Untrusted Enterprise Developer" when you try to open the app. You can trust the computer by setting it manually. Just go into **Settings > General > Device Management** and you will see an option to trust your certificate.

Once you have completed all of the brew installs in your terminal (), you have two options:

Deploy the same app to another iOS device

1. Connect the new device
2. From your Flutter project directory, run this file *open ios/Runner.xcworkspace* in a terminal window.
3. Select the connected device on Xcode
4. Everything should already be set up and ready to run, just set up trust on your device and you're done!

Deploy a new app

1. Connect the device
2. Again, you should run the following file: *open ios/Runner.xcworkspace* in a terminal window from project directory.
3. Select the connected device on Xcode. The center and side panels may be empty.
4. Click *Runner* on the left panel. This should populate the center and side panels.
5. Edit the "Bundle Identifier" so that it is a unique string. Remember that the bundle identifier is located in the

general tab under identities. If it is not unique, you will get an error at the next step.
6. Click on the *Signing and Capabilities* tab located at the center. Some versions of Xcode entitles it SigningThe tab may be titled "Signing" depending on your version of Xcode.
7. Select your team
8. Click on the "run Flutter app" in the terminal
9. You may or may not need to set up trusts with your device. However, if you do, then follow the steps enumerated in item 4 of troubleshooting above and you're done.

Chapter 4 Tip – Habit Building With The Calendar Trick

In this chapter, you learnt how to configure both your Android device and your computer for USB debugging. Also, you learnt how to establish an ADB connection through Wi-Fi.

It is very important that you see how your app behaves on various physical devices. This is critical if you plan to publish your app on Google Play. Why? Android devices tend to have quirks and limitations. If you don't check them, they can cause your app to behave in an odd manner, or even crash.

Chapter Summary

- Running your app on a physical device has been our point of focus in this chapter. It really taught us that when developing an Android application, it's crucial to test it on a real device. Apart from that, you need to prepare your development environment and also set up your Android for testing and debugging.
- It's time to explore the next item on the list. How to build beautiful user interfaces using Flutter widgets. Come along as

we break this topic into smaller bits of information you can grab fast.

Chapter Five: How to Build Beautiful UIs with Flutter Widgets

Flutter is used for creating high-performance as well as high-fidelity mobile applications for both iOS and Android. Also, it is a framework that makes it possible for a developer to build user interfaces that react smoothly in your application, while minimizing the amount of programming needed to synchronize and update your app's view.

Flutter makes it easy to get started building beautiful apps, with its rich set of Material Design and iOS widgets and behaviors. Your users will be interested in your app's natural look and feel, as Flutter uses features that are specific to your platform such as scrolling, fonts, and navigational patterns, among others. You'll feel productive with Flutter's practical-reactive framework.

In this chapter, I will guide you to build beautiful user interfaces (UIs) with Flutter widgets.

5.1 A One Screen Personal Business Card App - Micard

Micard is a personal business card. Just imagine every time you want to give someone your contact information, you'll eventually end up stocking multiple business cards in your pocket or purse. This might cause an awkward feeling anytime you don't have them on you. Well, now you can get people to download your business card as an app on their phone with all your details in it. By building it, you'll learn how to lay out UI on screen using various Flutter layout widgets.

Go to this url: https://github.com/londonappbrewery/mi_card_Flutter once you're ready. As you are here, you will discover skeletal projects for this coming module. There are icons and images sources that you will use to accomplish tasks here.

Clone it unto your local system by clicking on the green button 'CLONE or DOWNLOAD.' Click on the drop-down button to copy the url of that repository. Then, open up Android studio and select 'check out project from version control', select git as the provider. Paste the url you just copied and choose the location where you want the project to be saved. Click on clone for it to download that starter file and put it on your computer. When you get a pop up window, click on no.

Now, open up an existing Android studio project, navigate to where you've cloned that previous project by selecting Android studio projects or the right location where you initially saved the project on. Select the folder "mi_card_Flutter" and click open, Android studio will open it as a Flutter project. Click on "get dependencies", to clear any errors or warnings.

5.2 The Flutter Power Tools - Hot Reload and Hot Restart

For someone who is new to coding and technical jargon, the concepts of hot reload and hot restart is quite difficult. Maybe you had lots of issues understanding how hot reload and hot restart work when you tried your hands on them for the first time. Well, be glad as I have finally figured a way to understand them better.

The role of Flutter's hot reload feature is to assist you to quickly and easily test and create user interfaces, experiment, fix bugs, and even add features. It works by introducing up-to-date source code files into the Dart Virtual Machine. The Virtual Machine will then update classes with new forms of functions and fields. Lastly, the Flutter framework recreates the widget tree, which permits you to quickly see the effects of your changes.

Real World Example

Let's say that your job has made you a nomad, always travelling every weekend to another location for a function – business, meeting, conference, etc.

This means that you'll be packing your travel box anew every weekend you wish to travel. The truth of the matter is that it requires time to pack because if you do it hurriedly, you may end up forgetting many important things. So, what do you do?

All you should do is get a travel bag and pack up the very basic things that you would need anytime you travel, such as a toothbrush, toothpaste, towel, nightwear, shorts, and toilet soap. These are the basic things that will make you comfortable anytime you travel, right?

Now, suppose that you get a call from a friend inviting you to her wedding next weekend. Would you need to unpack all the contents of your bag to add a dress and probably a pair of shoes or would you just open your bag and add them? Remember you'll still need the basic things. The right thing to do is to simply add the dress and shoe instead of emptying the entire bag!

You can relate this scenario to hot reload and hot restart.

The function of hot reload is quite similar to just adding the dress. Hot reload implements the change in your UI in a couple of seconds, without reloading the whole app or messing with inputs and variables.

Hot restart, on the other hand, saves time by just implementing the functionality based on the closest build class in less than 10 seconds without restarting the whole app. Restarting the whole app would have done the same thing, but it would have done it in 40 seconds. Therefore, Hot restart saves developers time.

Hot restart consumes a lot of time in contrast to hot reload. However, it damages or recreates the state value and rebuilds it to the default. The app widget tree rebuilds completely with a newly typed code. This takes about 23 to 30 seconds compared with the default app restart time.

Now, you will be traveling on the weekend and all you have to do is load a dress into your box. If there's a need to add a pair of shoes, all you need do is open your box and put them in without rearranging the whole box.

How to perform hot reload in your app

1. Run the app from a supported Flutter editor such as Android studio or a terminal window. You can use a physical or virtual device as your target. Remember that you can run hot reload only on Flutter apps in debug mode.

2. Change one of the Dart files in your project. Most types of code modifications can be hot reloaded.

3. If you're working in an IDE/editor that supports Flutter's IDE tools, select Save All, or click the hot reload button on the toolbar.

If you're running the app at the command line using Flutter run, type r and press enter key in the terminal window.

After a successful hot reload operation, you'll see a message in the console like the one below.

Performing hot reload…

Reloaded 1 of 448 libraries in 978ms.

5.3 How to Use Container Widgets

Container is a parent or convenience widget that contains a child widget and controls it such as background, width, height, etc. It combines common sizing widgets, positioning and painting and can be used to add some styling properties.

Now, we need to create a page to contain the *Container* before using it. So, let's go ahead and create ContainPage in the form of a code structure that displays our code.

class ContainerPage extends StatefulWidget {

```
@override
State<StatefulWidget> createState() => _ContainerState();
}

class _ContainerState extends State<ContainerPage> {
@override
Widget build(BuildContext context) {
return Scaffold(
appBar: AppBar(
title: Text(PageName.CONTAINER),
),
body: SingleChildScrollView(
child: Column(
crossAxisAlignment: CrossAxisAlignment.start,
children: <Widget>[
Text("Hello World")
],
)),
);
}
}
```

What we're trying to achieve using the code above is to know that we will code in the *children* of *columns* such as *Text("Hello world")*. See the code below:

Column(

children: <Widget>[

Text("Hello World")

],

)

The output looks like this:

The truth is that it's very simple to use a container. So, if you really want to use it, all you have to do is to replace the Text("Hello World")

like the one written below. It contains a child with default parameters.

Container(

color: RED,

child: Text("Hello World"),

)

The output is:

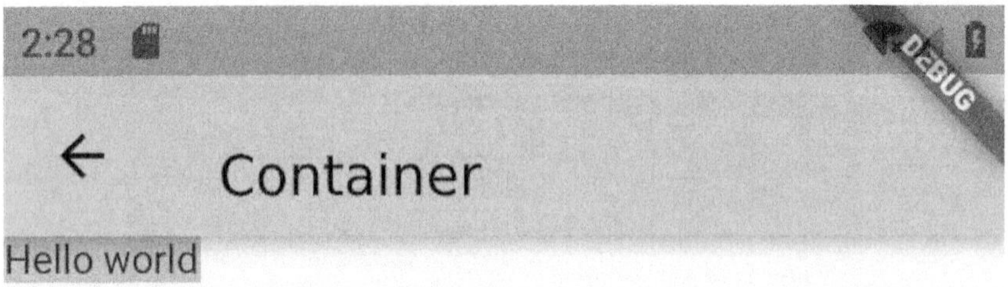

Let's look at the parameters of a container.

Constructor of the container

Container({

Key key,

this.alignment,

this.padding,

Color color,

Decoration decoration,

this.foregroundDecoration,

double width,

double height,

BoxConstraints constraints,

this.margin,

this.transform,

this.child,

})

Let's consider each property in detail below:

this.child:

This property is used to add a child widget for the container such as the *Text("My Kingdom")*. This parameter can only be used here if it is a widget.

Color color:

With this parameter, you can change the background color of the text. We can add a container with orange color. This coding is written below:

Container(

color: ORANGE,

child: Text("Color color"),

),

The output is:

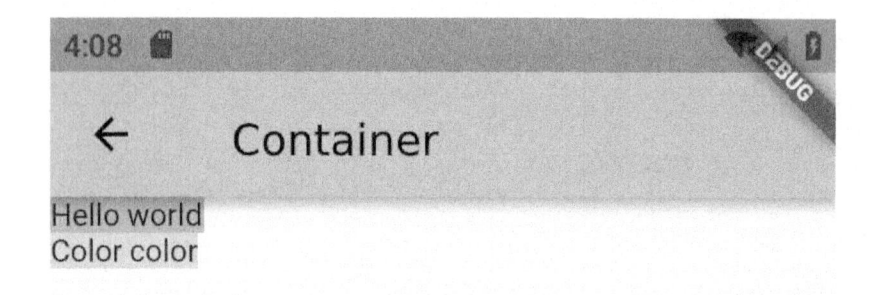

You should be careful with the color parameter as it cannot be used together with *"Decoration decoration"*. So, you can only use one parameter amongst the two of them.

this.padding:

This property is used to set *this.padding's* child distance from four directions. It is defined in the code below:

final EdgeInsetsGeometry padding;

Using the class extends *EdgeInsetsGeometry* is essential and we have only two choices in Flutter: *EdgeInsetsDirectional* and *EdgeInsets*. *EdgeInsetsDirectional* depends on the direction of *TextDirection*. On the other hand, *EdgeInsets* is dependent on the distance from top, bottom, left, and right. Here's the code:

Container(

color: YELLOW,

padding:

EdgeInsets.only(left: 10.0, right: 50.0, top: 10, bottom: 30),

child: Container(

color: BLUE_DEEP,

child: Text("this.padding"),

),
)

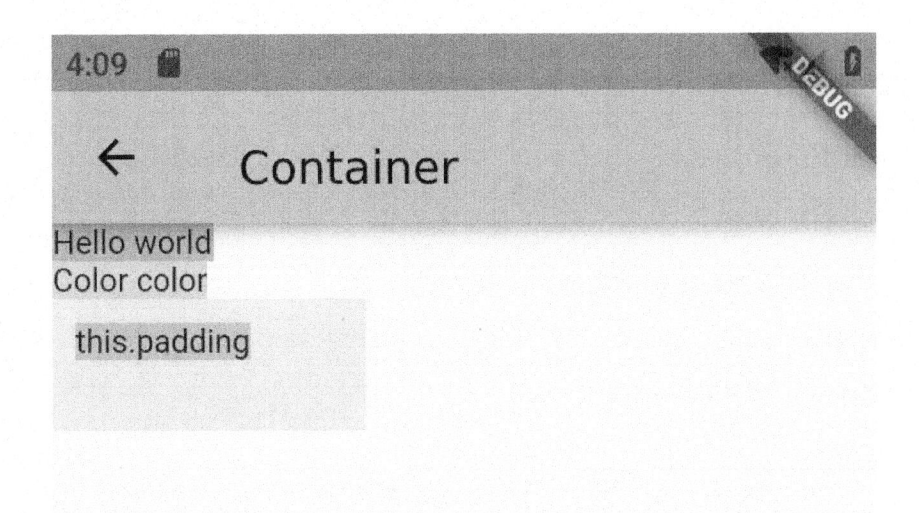

The arrow describes what is the top, bottom, left, and right for padding with *EdgeInsets*.

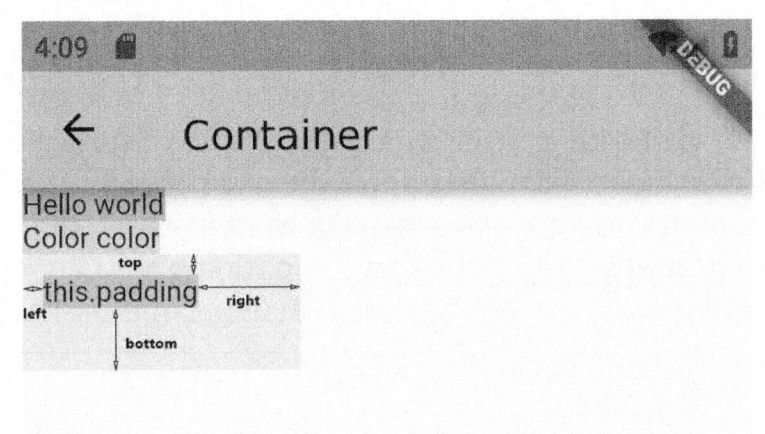

EdgeInsets have other functions and you can try them on your own. The example below will guide you.

EdgeInsets.all();

EdgeInsets.fromLTRB();

EdgeInsets.symmetric();

Width and height:

The widget will control its width and height using this two parameters:

double width,

double height,

Look at the following example:

Container(

width: 200.0,

height: 100.0,

color: GREEN,

child: Text("width = 200 , height = 100"),

),

this.margin:

This property is similar to **this.padding** parameter as both of them focus on the distance from the edge. However, there's a difference between them. If you look at define with margin parameter, you can see that the property is the same as the padding with *EdgeInsetsgeometry*. As a result, we can use *EdgeInsets*, too.

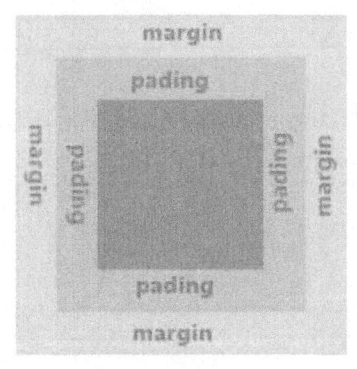

As usual, we define it in the code below:

final EdgeInsetsGeometry margin;

Here comes an example:

Container(

color: RED,

child: Container(

margin:

EdgeInsets.only(left: 10.0, right: 50.0, top: 10, bottom: 30),

color: GREEN,

child: Text("this.margin"),

),

),

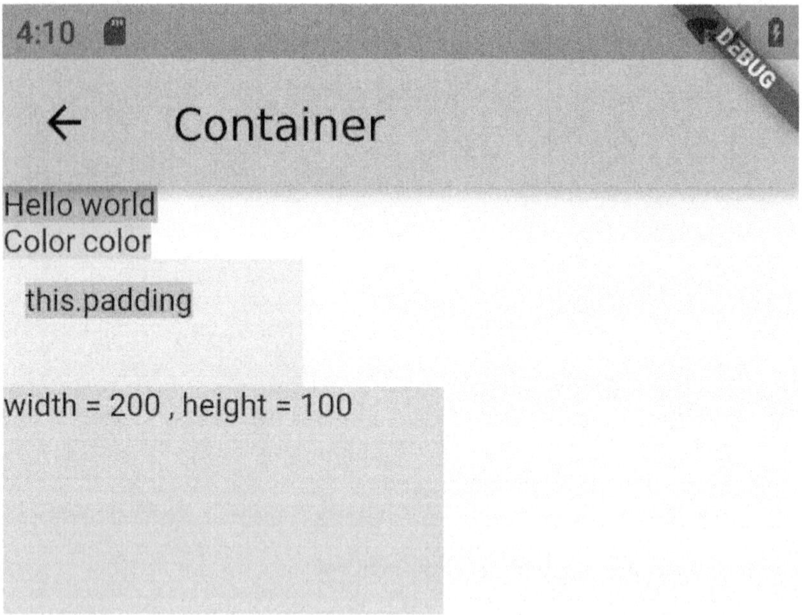
4:10
DEBUG
Container
Hello world
Color color
this.padding
width = 200 , height = 100

this.alignment:

In the same manner, define this in the code below:

final AlignmentGeometry alignment;

This property is not used directly. So, you should use the child class instead. There's a connection between *AlignmentGeometry*, *AlignmentDirectional*, and *Alignment*.

The *Alignment* has the following constant:

topLeft topCenter topRight

centerLeft center centerRight

bottomLeft bottomCenter bottomRight

In effect, the code below indicates that we're showing the child at the bottom-right of the *Container*.

Container(

color: BLUE_LIGHT,
alignment: Alignment.bottomRight,
height: 200,
child: Text("this.alignment"),
),

In the same way, you can use the *AlignmentDirectional* to display "locate your child" widget. We have the following constants as well.

topStart topCenter topEnd

centerStart center centerEnd

bottomStart bottomCenter bottomEnd

This is based on direction of *textDirection* and it is used the way the *Alignment* is used. The code is written below.

Container(

color: YELLOW,

height: 100.0,

alignment: AlignmentDirectional.bottomEnd,

child: Text(

"HellH",

textDirection: TextDirection.rtl,

),

)

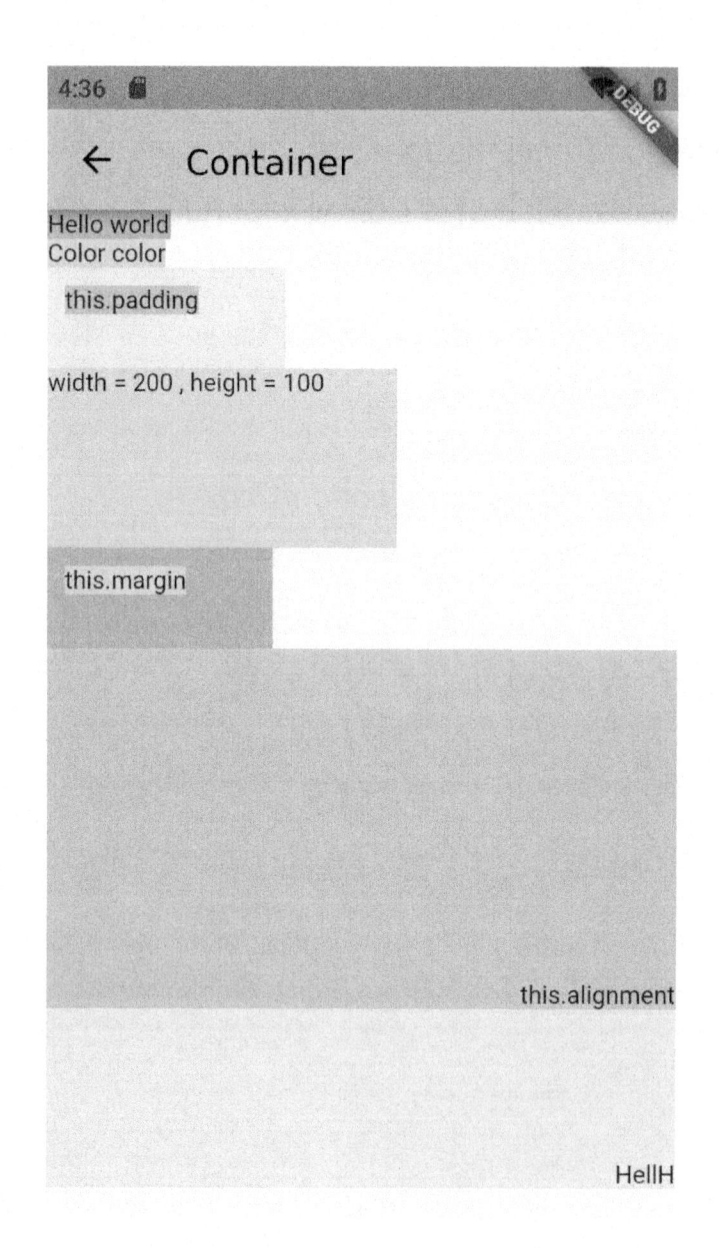

constraints:

The class of constraints is BoxConstraints, thus…

BoxConstraints constraints,

Constraints have many constructors including tight, loose, and expand. We'll focus on these three only.

tight

BoxConstraints.tight(Size size)

: minWidth = size.width,

maxWidth = size.width,

minHeight = size.height,

maxHeight = size.height;

If you assign a size to it, which has a fixed value to it, the minimum = maximum. You do not have to change the range.

loose

BoxConstraints.loose(Size size)

: minWidth = 0.0,

maxWidth = size.width,

minHeight = 0.0,

maxHeight = size.height;

You can view this constructor where the minimum = 0.0 and the maximum is the assigned value. So you give a maximum value to it if you assign a value..

expand

const BoxConstraints.expand({

double width,

double height

}): minWidth = width != null ? width : double.infinity,

maxWidth = width != null ? width : double.infinity,

minHeight = height != null ? height : double.infinity,

maxHeight = height != null ? height : double.infinity;

You can choose width, height or both. If you assign to it, minimum = maximum. If you do not assign, it will be equal to *infinity*, so it will be very large in the parent widget. At this juncture, here's an example using *expand*.

Container(

color: BLUE_LIGHT,

constraints: BoxConstraints.expand(height: 50.0),

child: Text("BoxConstraints constraints"),

),

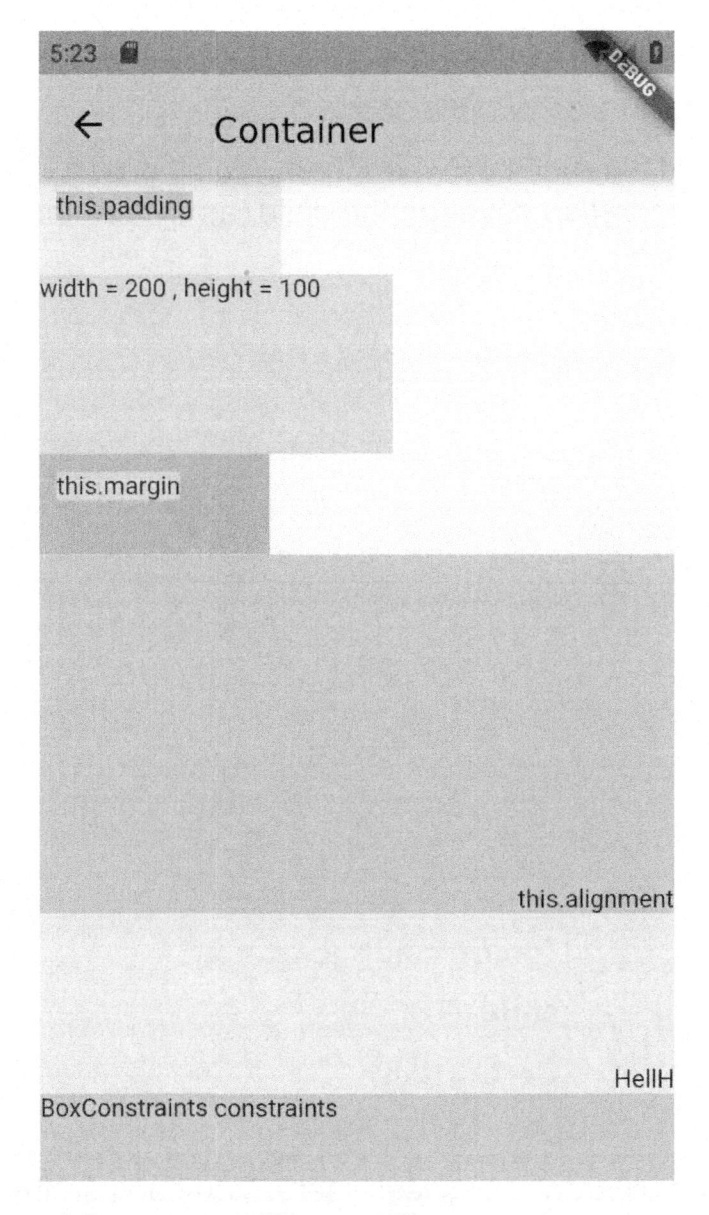

decoration and foregroundDecoration

There are two parameters here and they are the same type but have different effects.

Decoration decoration,

this.foregroundDecoration,

final Decoration foregroundDecoration;

Here are the differences between them. You'll observe the *foregroundDecoration* cover on the child, as well as the child on *decoration*.

■ **foregroundDecoration**
▫ child
▪ decoration

T is the major difference between them. You can use the *foregroundDecoration* the same way. The Decoration parameter cannot be used directly, you must use its child class. Let's look at the extent of its relationship with the two major classes.

Decoration extends to *BoxDecoration* and *ShapeDecoration.*

ShapeDecoration

The code is:

Container(

constraints: BoxConstraints.expand(height: 100.0),

padding: EdgeInsets.all(10),

decoration: ShapeDecoration(

shape: RoundedRectangleBorder(

borderRadius: BorderRadius.all(

Radius.circular(10.0),

),

),

color: RED),

child: Text("decoration: ShapeDecoration"),

)

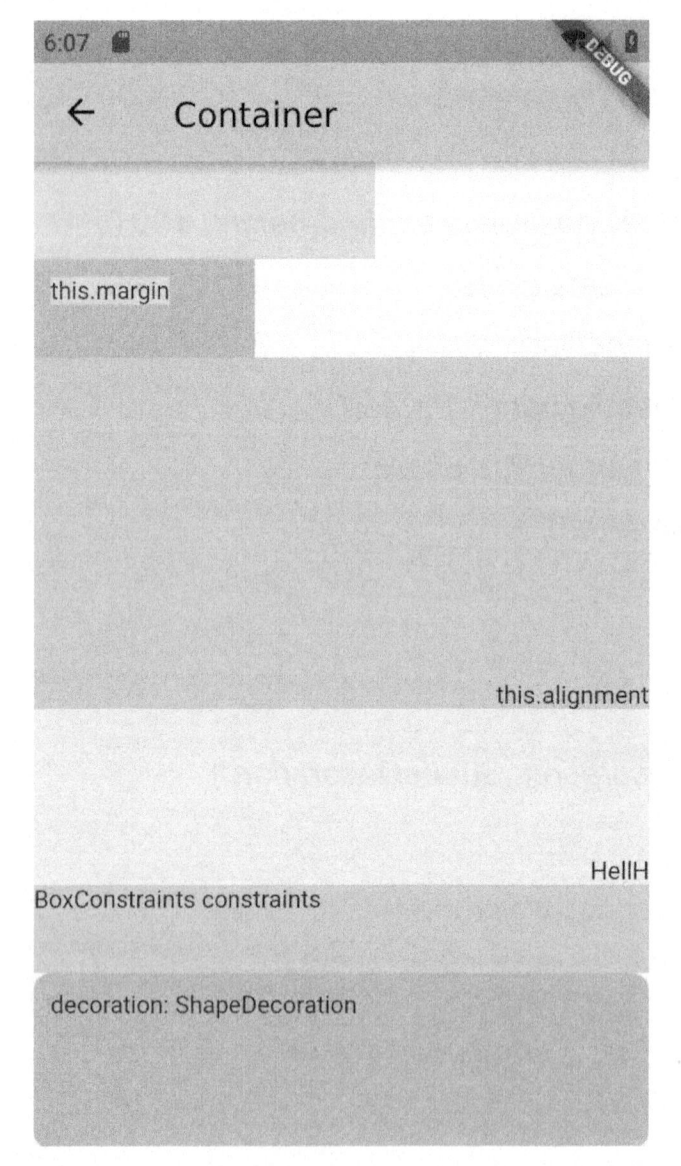

BoxDecoration

This code is:

Container(

constraints: BoxConstraints.expand(height: 200.0),

alignment: Alignment.center,

padding: EdgeInsets.all(10),

decoration: BoxDecoration(

gradient: LinearGradient(colors: [BLUE_LIGHT, YELLOW]),

shape: BoxShape.circle),

child: Text("decoration: BoxDecoration"),

),

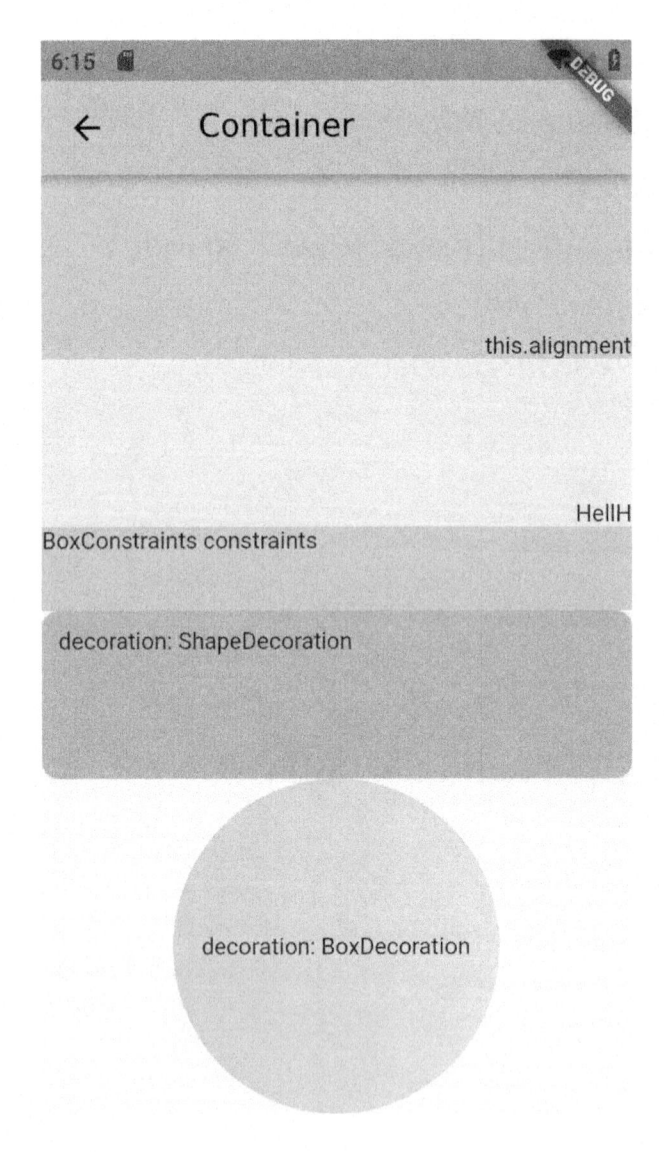

this.transform

The code is:

final Matrix4 transform;

This property is used to change the container coordinate in the parent widget. Since this parameter relates to math, it will be a bit difficult to explain.

```
Container(
  padding: EdgeInsets.only(top: 10, left: 10),
  constraints: BoxConstraints.expand(height: 100, width: 100),
  color: BLUE_LIGHT,
  child: Text("this.transform"),
),
Container(
  padding: EdgeInsets.only(top: 10, left: 10),
  constraints: BoxConstraints.expand(width: 100, height: 100),
  color: RED_LIGHT,
  transform: Matrix4.rotationY(pi / 4)..rotateX(pi / 4),
  child: Text("this.transform"),
)
```

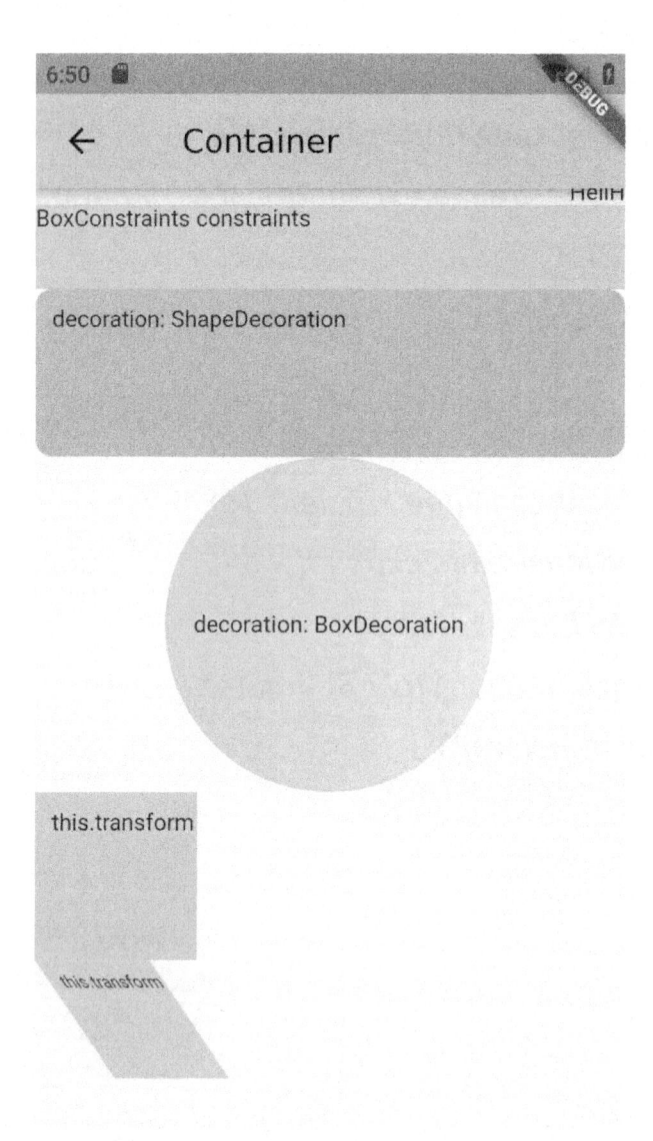

At this point, our container is complete, that's all you need. Just know there are some parameters you can use to complete your requirements and choose to use.

5.4 How You Can Use Column and Row Widgets for Layout

As usual, the first thing to do here is to create the ContainPage and put the whole code in it. So, open your dart terminal and type the following code:

```dart
import "package:Flutter/material.dart";
import 'package:Flutter_widgets/const/page_name_const.dart';
class RowColumnPage extends StatefulWidget {
@override
_RowColumnState createState() => _RowColumnState();
}
class _RowColumnState extends State<RowColumnPage> {
@override
Widget build(BuildContext context) {
return Scaffold(
appBar: AppBar(
title: Text(PageName.ROW_COLUMN),
),
body: SingleChildScrollView(
child: Column(
mainAxisAlignment: MainAxisAlignment.start,
children: <Widget>[
//our code here.
],
),
),
);
```

}

}

It will show a title just like this one below:

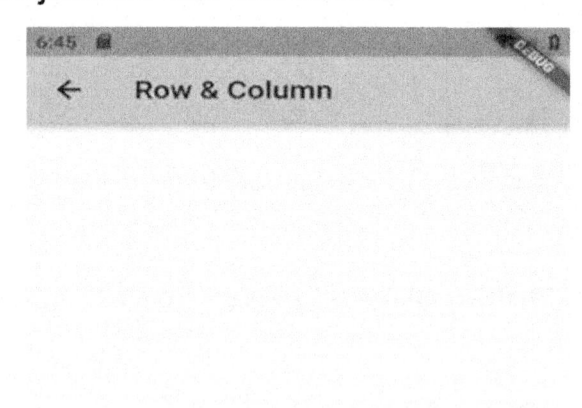

6:45 ← Row & Column

The output of the above code in a simulator is just the title, which is Row & Column.

As you can see from the code above, the widget contains a column. So, we can add two children *Text* in it. Just run the following code:

Column(

mainAxisAlignment: MainAxisAlignment.start,

children: <Widget>[

//our code here.

Text(

"Welcome to my Flutter Open.",

style: TextStyle(fontSize: TEXT_LARGE, color: GREEN),

),

Text(

"The developer is NieBin who is from China.",

style: TextStyle(fontSize: TEXT_NORMAL, color: BLUE_DEEP),

)

],

),

The outputs are the following two sentences:
- Welcome to my Flutter world.
- The developer is NieBin who is from China.

They come beneath Row & Column in the display terminal.

The row and column can show many widgets in one direction. The *Row* displays in the horizontal direction while the *Column* displays the vertical direction. Columns work the same way rows work. If you understand columns, then understanding rows won't be an issue.

Let us consider the constructor of a row and column in the following code.

For row:

Row({

Key key,

MainAxisAlignment mainAxisAlignment = MainAxisAlignment.start,

MainAxisSize mainAxisSize = MainAxisSize.max,

CrossAxisAlignment crossAxisAlignment = CrossAxisAlignment.center,

TextDirection textDirection,

VerticalDirection verticalDirection = VerticalDirection.down,

TextBaseline textBaseline,

List<Widget> children = const <Widget>[],

})

For column:

Column({

Key key,

MainAxisAlignment mainAxisAlignment = MainAxisAlignment.start,

MainAxisSize mainAxisSize = MainAxisSize.max,

CrossAxisAlignment crossAxisAlignment = CrossAxisAlignment.center,

TextDirection textDirection,

VerticalDirection verticalDirection = VerticalDirection.down,

TextBaseline textBaseline,

List<Widget> children = const <Widget>[],

})

You can see that both parameters are the same.

Also, you can control how a row or column aligns its children by using the *mainAxisAlignment* and *crossAxisAlignment* properties. For the row, the main axis runs on the horizontal direction and the cross axis runs vertically. For columns, the reverse is the case.

The *MainAxisAlignment* and *CrossAxisAlignment* parameters provide many constants for controlling alignment.

These two alignment categories can be set to one of the following values:

- **Start** - This places the children close to the start of the main axis based on the *textDirection*.
- **Center** - This positions the children as close to the middle of the main axis as possible.
- **End** - This positions the children as close to the middle of the main axis as possible depending on the textDirection.

spaceAround: Place the free space evenly between the children as well as half of that space before and after the first and last child.

spaceBetween: Place the free space evenly between the children.

spaceEvenly: Place the free space evenly between the children as well as before and after the first and last child.

You can try this by letting four widgets *Text* have name *open* in the *Row*. So, the *mainAxisAlignment* now becomes the parameter of the *_rowMainAlign(mainAxisAlignment)*. Here's the code:

Widget _rowMainAlign(mainAxisAlignment) => Container(

```
color: RED,
height: 50,
child: Row(
mainAxisAlignment: mainAxisAlignment,
children: <Widget>[
Text(
"Open",
style: TextStyle(color: TEXT_BLACK, fontSize: TEXT_NORMAL),
),
Text(
"Open",
style: TextStyle(color: TEXT_BLACK, fontSize: TEXT_NORMAL),
),
Text(
"Open",
style: TextStyle(color: TEXT_BLACK, fontSize: TEXT_NORMAL),
),
Text(
"Open",
style: TextStyle(color: TEXT_BLACK, fontSize: TEXT_NORMAL),
),
],
),
```

);

Then, apply a function to display all categories of the *mainAxisAlignment*. See below:

Widget _rowMainAlignAll() => Column(

children: <Widget>[

SizedBox(height: 10),

Container(

alignment: Alignment.topLeft,

child: Text(

"MainAxisAlignment.start",

style: TextStyle(color: TEXT_BLACK, fontSize: TEXT_LARGE),

),

),

_rowMainAlign(MainAxisAlignment.start),

SizedBox(height: 10),

Container(

alignment: Alignment.topLeft,

child: Text(

"MainAxisAlignment.center",

style: TextStyle(color: TEXT_BLACK, fontSize: TEXT_LARGE),

),

),

_rowMainAlign(MainAxisAlignment.center),

```
SizedBox(height: 10),
Container(
alignment: Alignment.topLeft,
child: Text(
"MainAxisAlignment.end",
style: TextStyle(color: TEXT_BLACK, fontSize: TEXT_LARGE),
),
),
_rowMainAlign(MainAxisAlignment.end),
SizedBox(height: 10),
Container(
alignment: Alignment.topLeft,
child: Text(
"MainAxisAlignment.spaceBetween",
style: TextStyle(color: TEXT_BLACK, fontSize: TEXT_LARGE),
),
),
_rowMainAlign(MainAxisAlignment.spaceBetween),
SizedBox(height: 10),
Container(
alignment: Alignment.topLeft,
child: Text(
"MainAxisAlignment.spaceEvenly",
```

```
      style: TextStyle(color: TEXT_BLACK, fontSize: TEXT_LARGE),
    ),
  ),
  _rowMainAlign(MainAxisAlignment.spaceEvenly),
  SizedBox(height: 10),
  Container(
    alignment: Alignment.topLeft,
    child: Text(
      "MainAxisAlignment.spaceAround",
      style: TextStyle(color: TEXT_BLACK, fontSize: TEXT_LARGE),
    ),
  ),
  _rowMainAlign(MainAxisAlignment.spaceAround),
  ],
);
```

The outcome of this is:

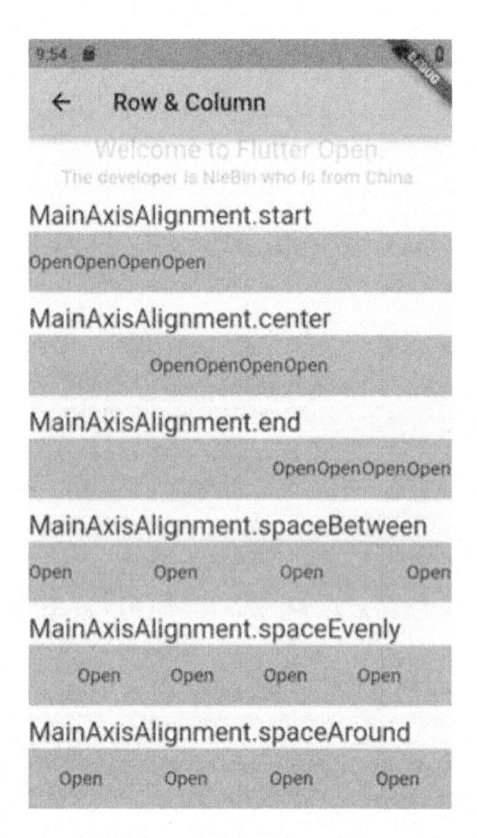

crossAxisAlignment is another feature that is helpful here, as its direction is the direction of the *mainAxisAlignment*. Thus, a great relationship exists between them. It has many types. We'll now write code by creating a function that has one parameter, but the same *Text*. Take a look at the following code:

Widget _crossAlign(crossAxisAlignment) => Container(

color: BLUE_LIGHT,

height: 80.0,

child: Row(

mainAxisAlignment: MainAxisAlignment.spaceEvenly,

crossAxisAlignment: crossAxisAlignment,

```
textBaseline: TextBaseline.ideographic,
children: <Widget>[
Text(
"Flutter",
style: TextStyle(color: TEXT_BLACK, fontSize: TEXT_NORMAL),
),
Text(
"Flutter",
style: TextStyle(color: TEXT_BLACK, fontSize: TEXT_NORMAL),
),
Text(
"Flutter",
style: TextStyle(color: TEXT_BLACK, fontSize: TEXT_NORMAL),
),
Text(
"Flutter",
style: TextStyle(color: TEXT_BLACK, fontSize: TEXT_NORMAL),
),
],
),
);
```

Since our CrossAxisAlignment.baseline requires the textBaseline, we just create a new one for it. Here you are:

```
Widget _crossBaseline(crossAxisAlignment, TextBaseline baseline)
=> Container(
color: BLUE_LIGHT,
height: 80.0,
child: Row(
mainAxisAlignment: MainAxisAlignment.spaceEvenly,
crossAxisAlignment: crossAxisAlignment,
textBaseline: baseline,
children: <Widget>[
Text(
"Flutter",
style: TextStyle(color: TEXT_BLACK, fontSize: TEXT_SMALL),
),
Text(
"Flutter",
style: TextStyle(color: TEXT_BLACK, fontSize: TEXT_NORMAL),
),
Text(
"Flutter",
style: TextStyle(color: TEXT_BLACK, fontSize: TEXT_LARGE),
),
Text(
"Flutter",
```

```
      style: TextStyle(color: TEXT_BLACK, fontSize: TEXT_NORMAL),
    ),
  ],
 ),
);
```

We can use the two of them together in the following code:

```
Widget _crossAlignAll() => Column(
  children: <Widget>[
    SizedBox(height: 10),
    Container(
      alignment: Alignment.topLeft,
      child: Text(
        "CrossAxisAlignment.center",
        style: TextStyle(color: TEXT_BLACK, fontSize: TEXT_LARGE),
      ),
    ),
    _crossAlign(CrossAxisAlignment.center),
    SizedBox(height: 10),
    Container(
      alignment: Alignment.topLeft,
      child: Text(
        "CrossAxisAlignment.end",
        style: TextStyle(color: TEXT_BLACK, fontSize: TEXT_LARGE),
```

```
        ),
      ),
      _crossAlign(CrossAxisAlignment.end),
      SizedBox(height: 10),
      Container(
        alignment: Alignment.topLeft,
        child: Text(
          "CrossAxisAlignment.start",
          style: TextStyle(color: TEXT_BLACK, fontSize: TEXT_LARGE),
        ),
      ),
      _crossBaseline(CrossAxisAlignment.start, null),
      SizedBox(height: 10),
      Container(
        alignment: Alignment.topLeft,
        child: Text(
          "CrossAxisAlignment.baseline.ideographic",
          style: TextStyle(color: TEXT_BLACK, fontSize: TEXT_LARGE),
        ),
      ),
      _crossBaseline(CrossAxisAlignment.baseline, TextBaseline.ideographic),
      SizedBox(height: 10),
```

```
Container(
alignment: Alignment.topLeft,
child: Text(
"CrossAxisAlignment.stretch",
style: TextStyle(color: TEXT_BLACK, fontSize: TEXT_LARGE),
),
),
_crossBaseline(CrossAxisAlignment.stretch, null)
],
);
```

The result is shown below:

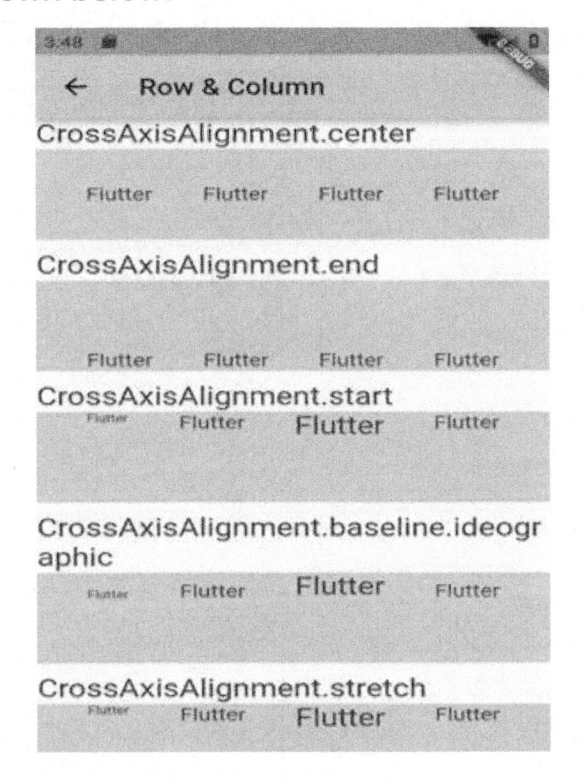

Another parameter to consider here is the *mainAxisSize*. It controls the space of the *Row* or *Column* and *mainAxisSize.min*, as well as sets the space to min and max for both *mainAxisSize.min* and *mainAxisSize.max*, respectively. So, we define a function to use it below:

Widget _mainSize(mainSize) => Container(

color: mainSize == MainAxisSize.min ? YELLOW : RED_LIGHT,

child: Row(

mainAxisSize: mainSize,

children: <Widget>[

Text(

"Nie",

style: TextStyle(color: TEXT_BLACK, fontSize: TEXT_SMALL),

),

Text(

"Nie",

style: TextStyle(color: TEXT_BLACK, fontSize: TEXT_NORMAL),

),

Text(

"Nie",

style: TextStyle(color: TEXT_BLACK, fontSize: TEXT_LARGE),

),

Text(

"Nie",

style: TextStyle(color: TEXT_BLACK, fontSize: TEXT_NORMAL),

),

],

));

Use the parameter by typing the following code in your terminal:

    _mainSize(MainAxisSize.min),

    _mainSize(MainAxisSize.max),

The result is:

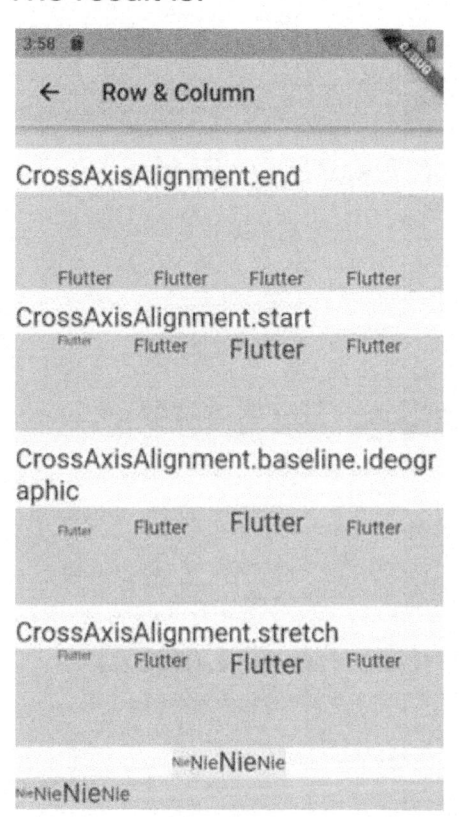

The verticalDirection is a parameter that is used in the vertical to control the direction of children widgets. Using the column, the following code can illustrate this parameter.

```
Widget _rowVertical(direct) => Container(
color: direct == VerticalDirection.down ? BLUE_DEEP : GREEN,
height: 100,
child: Column(
: direct,
mainAxisSize: MainAxisSize.max,
children: <Widget>[
Text(
"Bin",
style: TextStyle(color: TEXT_BLACK, fontSize: TEXT_SMALL),
),
Text(
"Bin",
style: TextStyle(color: TEXT_BLACK, fontSize: TEXT_SMALL),
),
Text(
"Bin",
style: TextStyle(color: TEXT_BLACK, fontSize: TEXT_LARGE),
),
Text(
"bin",
style: TextStyle(color: TEXT_BLACK, fontSize: TEXT_LARGE),
```

),
],
),
);

If you apply it as usual using the code below:

rowVertical(VerticalDirection.down),

_rowVertical(VerticalDirection.up),

the outcome is:

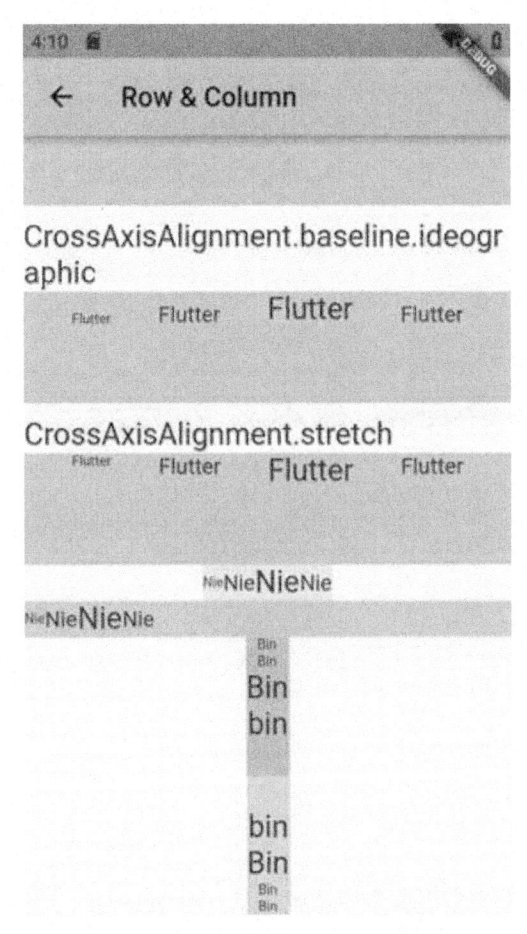

Closely related to verticalDirection is another parameter called textDirection. It is used in a horizontal direction as opposed to verticalDirection. The two ontrol the start direction of the drawing of children widgets. Take a look at the following code:

Widget _rowDirection(textDirect) => Container(

color: textDirect == TextDirection.ltr ? RED_LIGHT : PURPLE,

child: Row(

textDirection: textDirect,

children: <Widget>[

Text(

"Bin",

style: TextStyle(color: TEXT_BLACK, fontSize: TEXT_SMALL),

),

Text(

"Bin",

style: TextStyle(color: TEXT_BLACK, fontSize: TEXT_SMALL),

),

Text(

"Bin",

style: TextStyle(color: TEXT_BLACK, fontSize: TEXT_LARGE),

),

Text(

"bin",

style: TextStyle(color: TEXT_BLACK, fontSize: TEXT_LARGE),

),

],

),

);

Applying it, produces the following:

_rowDirection(TextDirection.ltr),

_rowDirection(TextDirection.rtl),

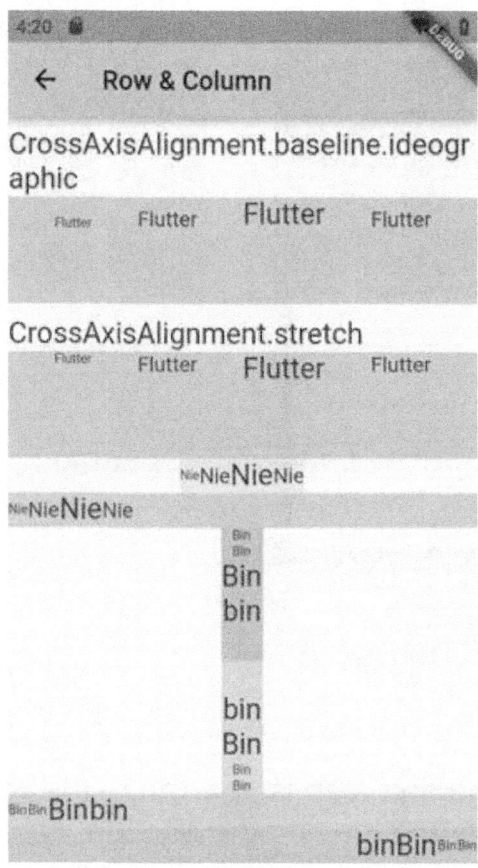

This is all you need to know about row and column widgets. The main parameters are *mainAxisAlignment* and *crossAxisAlignment*. If you understand these, others will be easy.

5.5 Flutter Layout Challenge

The aim of Flutter Layout Challenges is to attempt to recreate a specific app UI or design in Flutter.

This challenge will attempt Cupertino widgets and a simple custom drawer for iOS. Note that the aim here is to focus on the UI rather than actually fetching data from a backend server.

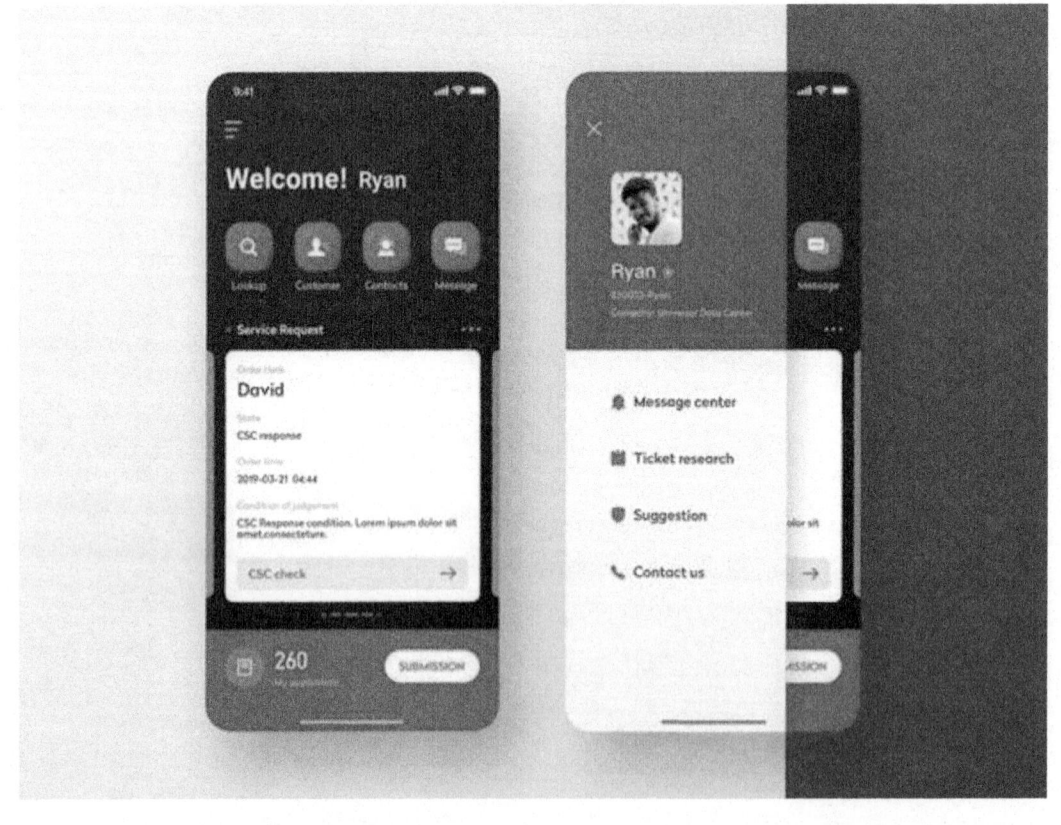

First things, first. The first step is to arrange the **main.dart** file by removing everything and leaving the **MyApp** class only. It's not necessary to keep the debug banner. So, remove it and add the **HomePage** widget as your home.

The code below accomplishes this:

```dart
import 'package:Flutter/material.dart';
import 'package:wg_by_sarah_d/home_page.dart';
void main() => runApp(MyApp());
class MyApp extends StatelessWidget {
  @override
  Widget build(BuildContext context) {
        return MaterialApp(
      title: 'Flutter Demo',
      debugShowCheckedModeBanner: false, // Remove the debug banner
      theme: ThemeData(
      primarySwatch: Colors.blue,
      ),
      home: HomePage(),
          );
  }
}
```

Here are some instructions. On the **home_page.dart** file, you'll create a **StatefulWidget**. Using the **initState()** approach, call **SystemChrome.setSystemUIOverlayStyle()** to make the status bar transparent. Use the following code:

```dart
@override
void initState() {
  SystemChrome.setSystemUIOverlayStyle(
```

SystemUiOverlayStyle(statusBarColor: Colors.transparent),

  );

  super.initState();

}

At last, we return a **CupertinoPageScaffold** on the **build** method and set its **backgroundColor** to **#2B292A**. That's all for now!

@override

Widget build(BuildContext context) {

  return CupertinoPageScaffold(

        backgroundColor: Color(0xFF2B292A),

  );

}

Layout of the App

To lay out the design on our Flutter app, we'll consider the following.

- **Navigation Bar**

The child of our scaffold will contain a **Stack**. The first child is a **CupertinoNavigationBar** having the same background color as the scaffold together with the menu icon on the left. Enclose it inside a **Positioned** widget to place it at the top of the screen.

Take note that the menu icon is not available in **CupertinoIcons**. Actually, the font file has it but it's hidden. Therefore we decided to use the Cupertino icons map. This is the code:

child: Stack(

  children: <Widget>[

```
        Positioned(
      top: 0.0,
      left: 0.0,
      right: 0.0,
      child: CupertinoNavigationBar(
      backgroundColor: Color(0xFF2B292A),
      border: Border.all(
        style: BorderStyle.none,
      ),
      actionsForegroundColor: Colors.white,
      leading: Icon(IconData(0xF394, fontFamily:
CupertinoIcons.iconFont, fontPackage:
CupertinoIcons.iconFontPackage)),
      ),
        ),
    ],
),
```

- **Welcome Text**

The next step is to include a **Container** to the **Stack** after the navigation bar. Again, enclose it inside a **Positioned** widget and give it a distance of 85 dp from the top. This will create room for the navigation bar.

This **Container** will have full width. Then, the height should take the height of the screen minus the height of the screen divided by 1.8. This will be the size of the slides below minus 120 dp (the height of the bottom red section).

The **Container** houses a **Column** whose first child is the welcome text. Let's see the code:

```
child:  Stack(
  children: <Widget>[
          Positioned(
          top: 90.0,
          left: 0.0,
          right: 0.0,
          child: Container(
          width: double.infinity,
          height: MediaQuery.of(context).size.height - (MediaQuery.of(context).size.height / 1.8) - 120.0,
          child: Padding(
          padding: const EdgeInsets.symmetric(horizontal: 20.0),
          child: Column(
          crossAxisAlignment: CrossAxisAlignment.start,
          mainAxisSize: MainAxisSize.max,
          children: <Widget>[
              RichText(
              textAlign: TextAlign.start,
              text: TextSpan(
              children: [
              TextSpan(
              text: 'Welcome! ',
```

```
                    style: TextStyle(
                        fontWeight: FontWeight.w500,
                        fontSize: 26.0,
                      ),
                    ),
                    TextSpan(
                    text: 'Ryan',
                    style: TextStyle(
                        fontSize: 20.0,
                      ),
                    ),
                    ]           ),
                   ),
             ],
           ),
          ),
          ),
                ),
      ],
    ),
```

Note: We used a **RichText** widget to be able to use different styles. So, you can use other ways to achieve the same purpose.

- **Buttons**

These four buttons will be placed in a **Row** widget. For now, we'll use the **Placeholder** widget to quickly mockup this section.

Having created a new **StatelessWidget**, we'll call it **SquareButton**. It's just a **Column** with a **Placeholder** for the button and another for the text, with a small space between them.

```
class SquareButton extends StatelessWidget {
  @override
  Widget build(BuildContext context) {
    return Column(
      mainAxisSize: MainAxisSize.min,
      children: <Widget>[
        Placeholder(
          color: Colors.red,
          fallbackWidth: 60.0,
          fallbackHeight: 60.0,
        ),
        SizedBox(
          height: 8.0,
        ),
        Placeholder(
          color: Colors.white,
          fallbackWidth: 60.0,
          fallbackHeight: 20.0,
        ),
```

```
      ],
    );
  }
}
```

The next step is to add a Row below the **RichText**, with four **SquareButton** inside. We want them to occupy the space proportionally and also align to the left and right to make it true to the design. The solution is very simple, just use **MainAxisAlignment.spaceBetween**.

```
... // RichText here in the same Column
Row(
    mainAxisSize: MainAxisSize.max,
    mainAxisAlignment: MainAxisAlignment.spaceBetween,
    children: <Widget>[
            SquareButton(),
            SquareButton(),
            SquareButton(),
            SquareButton(),
    ],
),
```

- **Service Request**

This is just a simple Row. Those small dots at the beginning are a **Container** with a **BoxDecoration**. Next to it goes a **Text** and finally an **Icon** which is called *ellipsis*.

```
Padding(
  padding: const EdgeInsets.only(bottom: 16.0),
  child: Row(
          crossAxisAlignment: CrossAxisAlignment.center,
          mainAxisSize: MainAxisSize.max,
          children: <Widget>[
     Container(
     width: 7.0,
     height: 7.0,
     decoration: BoxDecoration(
     color: Color(0xFFB42827),
     borderRadius: BorderRadius.circular(5.0),
     ),
     ),
      SizedBox(
      width: 8.0,
      ),
      Text(
      'Service Request',
        style: Theme.of(context).textTheme.subtitle.copyWith(color: Colors.white),
          ),
        Expanded(child: SizedBox()), // Make a separation between widgets
```

```
        Icon(
        CupertinoIcons.ellipsis,
        color: Colors.white,
        ),
            ],
    ),
  ),
),
```

Finally, change the alignment of the **Column** for better use of the space using the following codes below:

```
child: Column(
  ... // Other properties
  mainAxisAlignment: MainAxisAlignment.spaceAround,
  ... // Children widgets
),
```

- **Middle and Bottom Sections Container**

Now, let's add some containers for the other two sections.

```
Stack(
  children: [
        ... // Navigation bar
        ... // Welcome text and buttons
        Positioned(
    bottom: 120.0,
    left: 0.0,
```

right: 0.0,

child: Container(

height: MediaQuery.of(context).size.height / 1.8 - 90.0, // Substracting 90dp to compensate the height of status and navigation bars

),

),

Positioned(

bottom: 0.0,

left: 0.0,

right: 0.0,

child: Container(

height: 120.0,

color: Color(0xFFB42827),

),

),

],

),

- **Bottom Container**

The bottom container has a very simple content, using a **Row** for placing the items. So, we make the left icon by decorating a **Container** and placing an **Icon** centered inside.

Container(

width: 45.0,

```
          height: 45.0,
          decoration: BoxDecoration(
                    borderRadius: BorderRadius.circular(25.0),
                    color: Colors.white.withOpacity(0.1),
          ),
          child: Center(
                    child: Icon(
               IconData(0xF391, fontFamily: CupertinoIcons.iconFont,
fontPackage: CupertinoIcons.iconFontPackage),
                    color: Colors.white,
                          ),
          ),
),
```
The following texts column will properly align the text:
```
Column(
   crossAxisAlignment: CrossAxisAlignment.start,
   mainAxisSize: MainAxisSize.min,
   children: <Widget>[
             Text(
         '260',
         style:
Theme.of(context).textTheme.headline.copyWith(fontWeight:
FontWeight.w500, color: Colors.white),
                 ),
```

```
        Text(
      'My application',
        style: Theme.of(context).textTheme.caption.copyWith(color: Colors.white.withOpacity(0.5)),
            ),
    ],
 ),
```

For the button on the right, kindly place an **Expanded** widget to push the button to the right. We've already removed some padding from the **CupertinoButton** to suit the design.

```
Expanded(child: SizedBox()),

CupertinoButton(
  color: Colors.white,
  borderRadius: BorderRadius.circular(30.0),
  padding: const EdgeInsets.symmetric(horizontal: 32.0),
  child: Text(
        'SUBMISSION',
        style: TextStyle(
      color: Color(0xFFB42827),
      fontWeight: FontWeight.w500,
            ),
  ),
  onPressed: () {},
),
```

Thus far, this is what we have created:

Welcome! Ryan

• Service Request

260
My application

SUBMISSION

Create the SquareButton Widget

We'll be using the font_awesome_Flutter package here. So, you need to add it now to your *pubspec.yam1*. The **Font Awesome** icon pack is a set of Flutter icons which includes free icons both regular, solid, and custom.

Here, we'll add two parameters to this **StatelessWidget**: the label **String** and the **Icon.**

final String label;

final Icon icon;

SquareButton({

　@required this.label,

　@required this.icon,

}) : assert(label != null),

　　　assert(icon != null);

Then replace the first **Placeholder** with a **SizedBox** that will expand the **CupertinoButton** that it encloses. Remove the padding from the button and put the **Icon** received, resizing it a little.

SizedBox(

　width: 60.0,

　height: 60.0,

　child: CupertinoButton(

　　　　padding: EdgeInsets.zero,

　　　　borderRadius: BorderRadius.circular(20.0),

　　　　onPressed: () {},

　　　　color: Color(0xFFB42827),

```
        child: Icon(icon.icon, size: 26.0,),
  ),
),
```

The label below is enclosed in a **Center** within a **Container** with the previous dimensions of the **Placeholder**.

```
Container(
  width: 60.0,
  height: 20.0,
  child: Center(
        child: Text(
    label,
        style: Theme.of(context).textTheme.caption.copyWith(color: Colors.white),
        ),
  ),
),
```

You can use the following code:

```
Row(
  mainAxisSize: MainAxisSize.max,
  mainAxisAlignment: MainAxisAlignment.spaceBetween,
  children: <Widget>[
        SquareButton(
      icon: Icon(FontAwesomeIcons.search),
      label: 'Lookup',
```

```
      ),
      SquareButton(
icon: Icon(FontAwesomeIcons.userAlt),
label: 'Customer',
      ),
      SquareButton(
icon: Icon(FontAwesomeIcons.headset),
label: 'Contacts',
      ),
      SquareButton(
icon: Icon(FontAwesomeIcons.solidComments),
label: 'Message',
      ),
   ],
),
```

Let's see what we've coded so far.

The Page Review

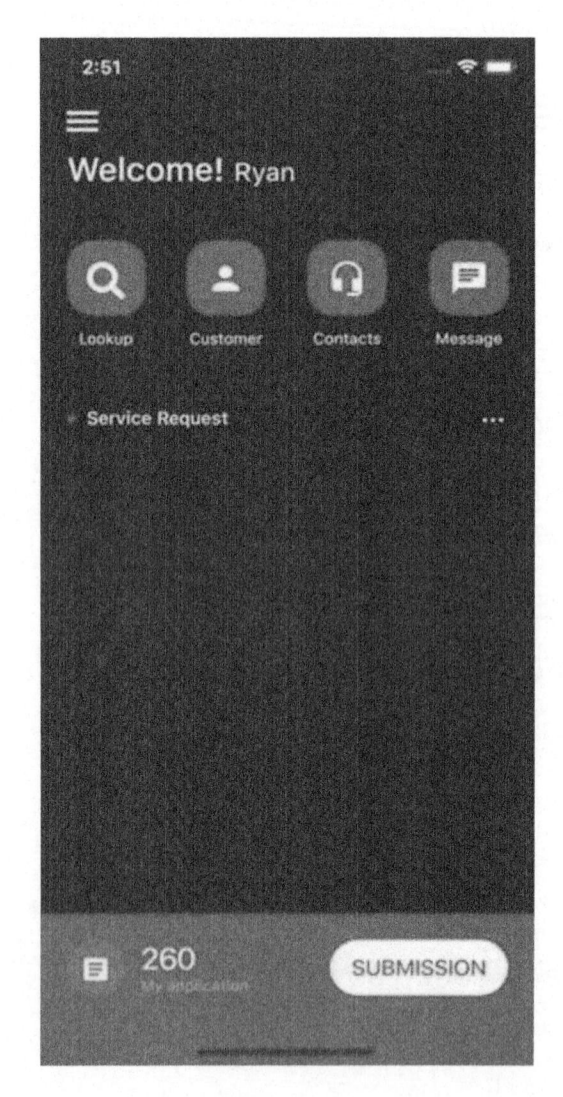

Begin the page review by creating a **PageViewCardListTile** widget that will be the content of the cards on the **PageView**.

This widget receives a title and a content value. Add a **biggerContent** bool (a Boolean variable is one whose value is either true or false) with a default value of false that will help handle the text in the design. Here's the code:

```dart
class PageViewCardListTile extends StatelessWidget {
    final String title;
    final String content;
    final bool biggerContent;

    PageViewCardListTile({
            @required this.title,
            @required this.content,
            this.biggerContent = false,
    }) : assert(title != null),
        assert(content != null);

    @override
    Widget build(BuildContext context) {
            return Column(
        mainAxisSize: MainAxisSize.min,
        crossAxisAlignment: CrossAxisAlignment.start,
        children: [
        Text(
        title,
        style: Theme.of(context).textTheme.caption,
        ),
        SizedBox(
```

```
        height: 4.0,
      ),
      Text(
        content,
        style: biggerContent ? Theme.of(context).textTheme.title : Theme.of(context).textTheme.subtitle,
      ),
    ],
      );
  }
}
```

Still on, we proceed to creating a **PageViewCard** widget that will contain these tiles made before.

```
class PageViewCard extends StatelessWidget {
  @override
  Widget build(BuildContext context) {
      return Padding(
    padding: const EdgeInsets.symmetric(horizontal: 7.0),
    child: Card(
     shape: RoundedRectangleBorder(
     borderRadius: BorderRadius.circular(15.0),
    ),
    margin: EdgeInsets.zero,
    child: Padding(
```

```
        padding: const EdgeInsets.all(16.0),
        child: Column(
        crossAxisAlignment: CrossAxisAlignment.start,
        mainAxisAlignment: MainAxisAlignment.spaceBetween,
        children: <Widget>[
            PageViewCardListTile(
            title: 'Order clerk',
            content: 'David',
            biggerContent: true,
            ),
            PageViewCardListTile(
            title: 'State',
            content: 'CSC response',
            ),
            PageViewCardListTile(
            title: 'Order time',
            content: '2019-03-21 04:44',
            ),
            PageViewCardListTile(
            title: 'Condition of judgement',
            content: 'CSC Response condition. Lorem ipsum dolor sit amet, consectetur.',
            ),
```

```
SizedBox(
    child: CupertinoButton(
    padding: const EdgeInsets.symmetric(horizontal: 16.0),
    child: Row(
    mainAxisSize: MainAxisSize.max,
    children: <Widget>[
    Text(
        'CSC check',
        style: TextStyle(
        color: Color(0xFFB42827),
        ),
    ),
    Expanded(child: SizedBox()),
        RotatedBox(
            quarterTurns: 3,
            child: Icon(
            CupertinoIcons.down_arrow,
            color: Color(0xFFB42827),
            ),
        ),
    ],
    ),
```

```
                    color: Colors.redAccent.withOpacity(0.3),
                    onPressed: () {},
                  ),
                )
              ],
            ),
          ),
        ),
      );
    }
}
```

The code above is straightforward, though very long. The only thing that is new, is the use of a **RotatedBox** to convert a down arrow icon, into a right arrow.

Now we need the **PageView**, which we will be adding as a child of the **Container** we defined before for this purpose.

Create a **PageController** setting with the **viewportFraction** to a value of 0.92. This will let you see the borders of the widgets on the left and right.

```
PageController _pageController = PageController(
  viewportFraction: 0.92,
  initialPage: 1,
);
```

Then clearly show this **PageView** and occupy it with some **PageViewCard** widgets. We're using a **Stack** as we need to put those position tracking lines up.

```
child:  Stack(
  children: <Widget>[
        Padding(
      padding: const EdgeInsets.only(bottom: 40.0),
       child: PageView(
      controller: _pageController,
      children: <Widget>[
      PageViewCard(),
      PageViewCard(),
      PageViewCard(),
      ],
      ),
            ),
  ],
),
```

Our interpretation of this widget's behavior might not be the identical to the original, but it should be very close.

Here is this widget's code:

```
class TrackingLines extends StatelessWidget {
  final int length;
  final int currentIndex;
```

```dart
TrackingLines({
    @required this.length,
    @required this.currentIndex,
}) : assert(length != null && length > 0),
    assert(currentIndex != null && currentIndex < length);

@override
Widget build(BuildContext context) {
    return Row(
    mainAxisSize: MainAxisSize.min,
    children: List.generate(length, (index) {
    return Padding(
     padding: const EdgeInsets.all(3.0),
     child: Container(
     width: currentIndex == index ? 15.0 : 10.0,
     height: 3.0,
     color: currentIndex == index ? Color(0xFFB42827) : Colors.grey,
        ),
        );
    }),
        );
}
```

}

It receives a length and the **currentIndex** and updates when the **currentIndex** matches the line index. For it to be updated, add a listener to the **PageController** on the **initState()** method.

_pageController.addListener(() {

   setState(() => _currentIndex = _pageController.page.round());

});

Also, put the **TrackingLines** widget within the same **Stack** with the **PageView**.

... // PageView here

Align(

   alignment: Alignment.bottomCenter,

   child: Padding(

            padding: const EdgeInsets.only(bottom: 16.0),

                child: TrackingLines(

      length: 5,

      currentIndex: _currentIndex,

              ),

   ),

),

So, let's see what it's looking like now.

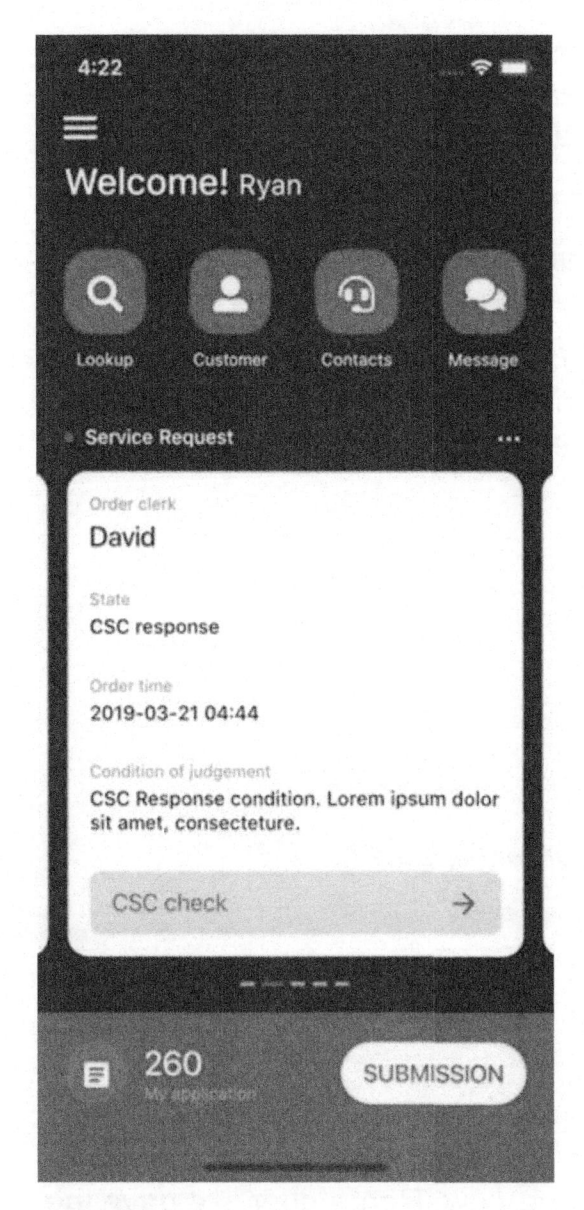

The Drawer

As we approach the end of this challenge, we're faced with a small problem. If you check the **CupertinoPageScaffold**, you'll see that it doesn't have a drawer property.

So, how do we go about creating this drawer? One option could be to combine the material **Scaffold** and **Drawer** widgets, with the other **Cupertino** widgets. There's also another way.

How to create the drawer layout

First of all, we'll create this layout and place it right in front of what we have now. That means, at the end of our main **Stack**.

So, add a **Container** and give it a full screen height as well as two-thirds of the screen width. Then, put it towards the end of the **Stack**. Give a white color and use **Positioned** to make it occupy the entire height of the screen.

Positioned(

　top: 0.0,

　bottom: 0.0,

　left: 0.0,

　child: Container(

　　　*width: (MediaQuery.of(context).size.width / 3) * 2,*

　　　height: double.infinity,

　　　color: Colors.white,

　),

),

Now, we need to divide it using the same number we've been using for the bottom container and the PageView. Remember, we gave the bottom container 120 dp in height, and the height of the screen divided by 1.8 minus 90 dp (because of the navigation bar) to the **PageView**. Therefore, we'll make the red section of the drawer with a height of the screen, minus height of the screen divided by 1.8, minus 90dp, minus 120dp. This will match perfectly with the position of the cards on the PageView.

Obviously, we'll use a Stack again.

child: Stack(

  children: <Widget>[

      Container(

    width: double.infinity,

    height: MediaQuery.of(context).size.height - (MediaQuery.of(context).size.height / 1.8 - 90.0) - 120.0,

    color: Color(0xFFB42827),

      ),

  ],

),

Here's what it looks like:

Animate the Drawer

Before continuing with the content within the drawer, we'll implement the animated open or close behavior.

Begin by replacing the **Positioned** widget with an **AnimatedPositioned** and give a **Duration** of 300 milliseconds.

Declare a variable **_isDrawerOpen** of type bool and initialize it with false. Then replace the left property with a ternary operator to change the position based on that variable.

AnimatedPositioned(

  duration: Duration(milliseconds: 300),

  top: 0.0,

  bottom: 0.0,

  *left: _isDrawerOpen ? 0.0 : -(MediaQuery.of(context).size.width / 3) * 2,*

  child: Container(

      ...

  ),

),

This will hide our drawer. Now, the next task to accomplish is to change the **_isDrawerOpen** value by tapping on the menu button.

On the navigation bar, enclose the **Icon** with a **GestureDetector** to be able to tap on it. Then use an anonymous function to change the state of the drawer.

leading: GestureDetector(

  onTap: () => setState(() => _isDrawerOpen = true),

  child: Icon(

      IconData(0xF394, fontFamily: CupertinoIcons.iconFont, fontPackage: CupertinoIcons.iconFontPackage),

  ),

),

Add a clear icon within the red section of the drawer to close the drawer.

```
Container(
    ... // Width and height
    color: Color(0xFFB42827),
    child: Stack(
            children: <Widget>[
        Positioned(
        top: 50.0,
        left: 10.0,
        child: GestureDetector(
        onTap: () => setState(() => _isDrawerOpen = false),
        child: Icon(
        CupertinoIcons.clear,
        color: Colors.white,
        size: 40.0,
        ),
        ),
        ),
            ],
    ),
),
```

We now have a working drawer! But the animation is too linear. Let's use a curve.

```
AnimatedPositioned(
  duration: Duration(milliseconds: 300),
  curve: Curves.easeIn,
  ...
),
```
Here's what it will look like:

I think this is much better, right?

Creating the Shadow

Since the drawer is flat, it needs to be shadowed.

Include a **BoxDecoration** to the white **Container** of the drawer, so that it will hold the **BoxShadow** for the drawer.

```
... // AnimatedContainer
child: Container(
  width: (MediaQuery.of(context).size.width / 3) * 2,
  height: double.infinity,
  decoration: BoxDecoration(
        color: Colors.white,
        boxShadow: [
    BoxShadow(
     color: Colors.black.withOpacity(0.3),
     blurRadius: 5.0,
    ),
        ],
  ),
  ...
),
```

Now, we're having a good shadow that will make the drawer stay above the main content.

The menu items list

Create a new widget called **MenuItem**. It will be used on the menu for displaying the navigation options. It's very simple, just an icon and text. Declare the parameters for this widget, and place the content in a Row.

```
class MenuItem extends StatelessWidget {
```

```
final Icon icon;
final String label;

MenuItem({
    @required this.icon,
    @required this.label,
}) : assert(icon != null),
    assert(label != null);

@override
Widget build(BuildContext context) {
    return Padding(
    padding: const EdgeInsets.only(bottom: 42.0),
    child: Row(
    crossAxisAlignment: CrossAxisAlignment.center,
    children: <Widget>[
    Icon(
     icon.icon,
     color: Color(0xFFB42827),
    ),
    SizedBox(
     width: 8.0,
    ),
```

```
            Text(
            label,
            style: TextStyle(
                fontWeight: FontWeight.w500,
            ),
          ),
        ],
      ),
        );
  }
}
```

You have to include another **Container** beneath the red one. There, you will be placing these menu options.

```
Align(
  alignment: Alignment.bottomCenter,
  child: Container(
        width: double.infinity,
    height: MediaQuery.of(context).size.height / 1.8 + 30.0,
        child: Padding(
      padding: const EdgeInsets.only(left: 46.0, top: 46.0),
      child: Column(
        children: <Widget>[
        MenuItem(
```

```
                  icon: Icon(FontAwesomeIcons.solidBell),
                  label: 'Message center',
                ),
                MenuItem(
                  icon: Icon(FontAwesomeIcons.clipboardList),
                  label: 'Ticket research',
                ),
                MenuItem(
                  icon: Icon(FontAwesomeIcons.shieldAlt),
                  label: 'Suggestion',
                ),
                MenuItem(
                  icon: Icon(Icons.phone),
                  label: 'Contact us',
                ),
              ],
            ),
          ),
        ),
      ),
```

Note that I'm hardcoding everything here. Obviously you won't want to do that on a real app.

User Information

For the user information on the top of the drawer, create a separated **StatelessWidget** and name it **UserInfo**.

We'll put the elements within a **Column**, starting with a **Card** where we will show the picture. We can get the rounded corners by enclosing the image in a **ClipRRect**. The **FadeInImage.network** will give us a good transition when loading the image.

The next elements are just some text, except for the little circle icon on the right of the name.

```
class UserInfo extends StatelessWidget {
    final String picture;
    final String name;
    final String id;
    final String company;

    UserInfo({
            @required this.picture,
            @required this.name,
            @required this.id,
            @required this.company,
    }) : assert(picture != null && name != null && id != null && company != null);

    @override
    Widget build(BuildContext context) {
            return Column(
```

```
mainAxisSize: MainAxisSize.min,
crossAxisAlignment: CrossAxisAlignment.start,
children: <Widget>[
Card(
 margin: EdgeInsets.zero,
 elevation: 2.0,
 shape: RoundedRectangleBorder(
  borderRadius: BorderRadius.circular(12.0),
 ),
 child: Container(
 width: 80.0,
 height: 80.0,
 child: ClipRRect(
        borderRadius: BorderRadius.circular(12.0),
        child: FadeInImage.assetNetwork(
        placeholder: picture,
        image: picture,
 ),
 ),
 ),
 ),
SizedBox(
 height: 9.0,
```

```
    ),
    Row(
     children: <Widget>[
      Text(
        name,
        style: Theme.of(context).textTheme.headline.copyWith(color: Colors.white),
      ),
      SizedBox(
        width: 8.0,
      ),
      Container(
        width: 12.0,
        height: 12.0,
        decoration: BoxDecoration(
         color: Colors.white.withOpacity(0.3),
         shape: BoxShape.circle,
        ),
        child: Center(
         child: Icon(
          CupertinoIcons.play_arrow_solid,
          size: 8.0,
          color: Colors.white,
```

```
            ),
          ),
        ),
      ],
    ),
    SizedBox(
      height: 6.0,
    ),
    Text(
      id,
      style: Theme.of(context).textTheme.caption.copyWith(color: Colors.white.withOpacity(0.6)),
    ),
    SizedBox(
      height: 6.0,
    ),
    Text(
      company,
      style: Theme.of(context).textTheme.caption.copyWith(color: Colors.white.withOpacity(0.6)),
    )
  ],
    );
}
```

}

The last step is to add this new widget, on the same **Stack** where the clear icon is, on the red section of the drawer.

```
Align(
  alignment: Alignment.bottomLeft,
  child: Padding(
        padding: const EdgeInsets.only(left: 46.0, bottom: 46.0),
        child: UserInfo(
      picture: 'https://shopolo.hu/wp-content/uploads/2019/04/profile1-%E2%80%93-kopija.jpeg',
      name: 'Ryan',
      id: '0023-Ryan',
      company: 'Universal Data Center',
        ),
  ),
),
```

And that's it!

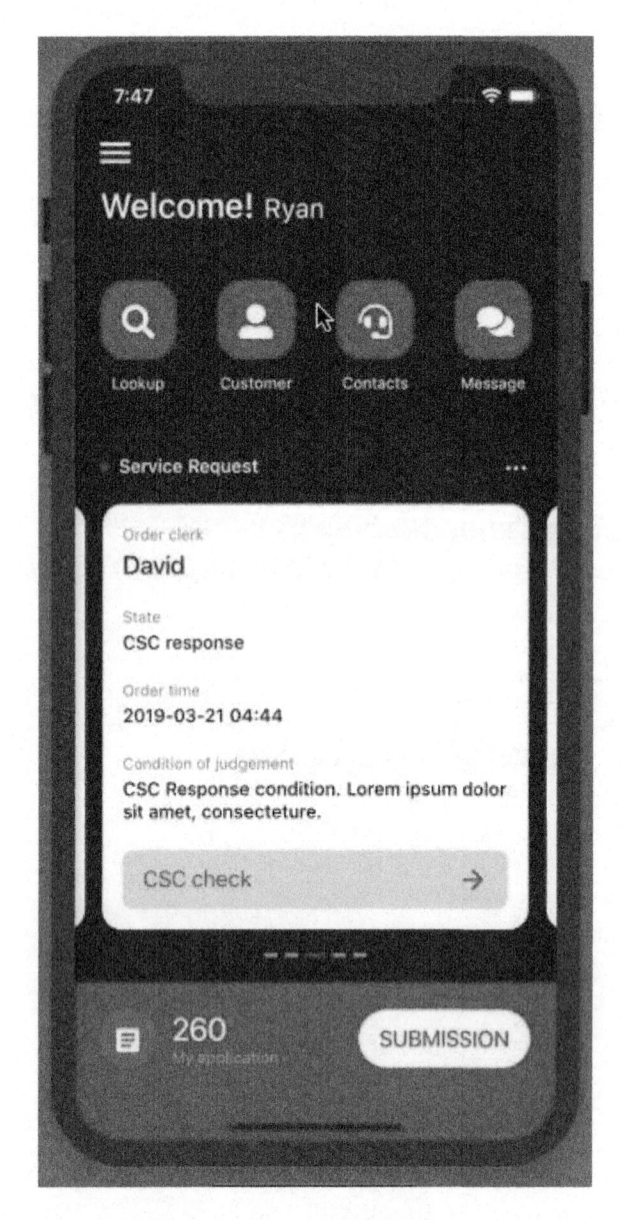

5.6 Tapping into the Widget Properties

Let's get started building our final product, which is our business card of sorts, but in an app form. You can attest to the fact that the layout goes from top to bottom. As a result, the most befitting layout widget that should be used is a column. Within the column, we'll have something that can show an image in a circle.

A little text that displays our name, a little information about our occupation and then a horizontal line to divide this top part from the bottom part. Looking at it, you'll see that it shows our phone number and contact details.

Let's get started making this using what we've just learned so far. Start with a column. The column, of course, needs to have a child parameter, and we need to decide which children we want inside it. The first child is going to be something called a CircleAvatar.

If you hover on CircleAvatar and wait for it, it'll show you the QuickDocs and it will tell you that if you choose it, you will get a circle that describes a user. It is used with a user profile image and the image will be cropped to have a circle shape.

So even though we're not really building a profile, in this case, it still makes sense to use this widget so that we get our image automatically filled into a circle. There's lots of these widgets that the Flutter team have created for common use cases such as building out a user profile.

What are the sort of things that we can put in a *CircleAvatar*?

Well, if you click on the *CircleAvatar* and if you're on a Mac, if you hit control J, or if you're in Windows, you hit control Q, you'll end up with the QuickDocs. So, the QuickDocs will show you how to configure the *CircleAvatar*. It will even show you how you can set its background color, its child, the things it contains, a background image, a foreground color, and the radius.

We're going to keep ours really simple, we're going to give it a radius and it's just going to be 50. So, this will come up just as a circle in the default blue color.

Now, what if I wanted to specify a color, let's give it a background color of red. So I can change all of these properties that I discovered in *QuickDocs*. Depending on what it is that you want to set for the radius or the image, you can customize your widgets. Instead of having a background color, as a challenge I want you to figure out how you can add a picture of yourself, or an image that you find on the internet inside the *CircleAvatar*.

So through the use of *QuickDocs* and what you've learned before, try and complete this challenge and see if you can turn it into a circle like this with your own custom picture. All right, I hope you gave that a go and you remembered how to do it. Here on my desktop I've got a picture of myself and I'm going to rename it to make my life a little bit easier.

I'm just going to call it Angela and I'm going to keep the extension; in this case the picture is a JPG. Then I'm going to go into my Flutter Project and I'm going to create a new directory. I'm going to call this Images.

So now I'm going to drag and drop my image into the Images folder and then click Okay when I get prompted. At this point, because we got our project off of GitHub, it asks us whether we want to track the changes that we're making to this project. Right, you can go ahead and click yes.

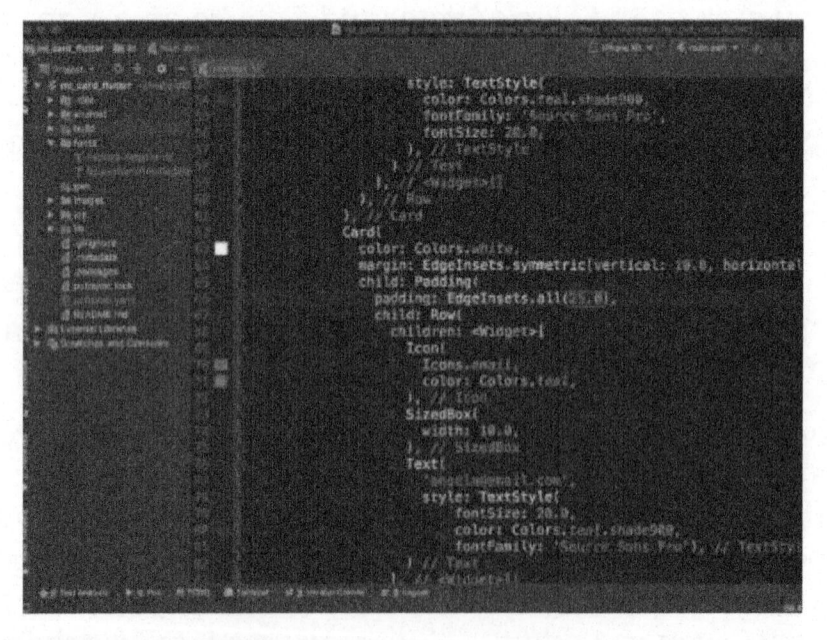

Here we've got our image and it's now inside our project, in a folder called Images. This is the perfect time to go into our *pubspec.yaml* and clean up a lot of these comments and then we can go ahead and add in the parts that we need.

So, remember the comments start with a pound sign or a hashtag. And try to not accidentally delete parts that are not comments, like the SDK. I'm going to select all of that and I'm going to hold down command or control and hit the forward slash button. Now, remember that our *pubspec.yaml* file is fragile about how we space it. So, the assets have to be on the same line as the uses-material-design because it's a child of our Flutter settings.

The image is going to be indented by two spaces. So, you can press the spacebar twice or tap the tab button if you want to. Now, inside our Images folder, I've got an image called Angela.JPG.

So, now we're ready to change our CircleAvatar. Instead of having a background color, we're going to have a background image instead.

Our image is going to be an *AssetImage* and the name of the image is, of course, images/Angela.JPG. Let's hit save and we should see our image show up in our little *CircleAvatar* here, brilliant. Did you manage to get that right?

If you have any trouble with the *AssetImage* and *pubspec.yaml*, be sure to review the lesson above about how to import images into our project assets, where we go into that in more detail.

Now that we've set up our CircleAvatar, the next step is to add our name to our business card. So, I'm going to add a text widget and my name. At this stage, you can see that the text shows up in the default layout, so it's just a piece of black text in the default font. What if we wanted to customize the styling of our text? Well, we can take a look at the piece of text, hit control J or control Q and see what other things that we can change about it. We can change the data that goes in, so in our case it's Angela Yu. We can change the style. So we have to set a property called style and it's going to be of type *TextStyle*. So let's try that. Let's add the style of property and let's change it to a *TextStyle*.

Now what kind of things can we do with *TextStyle*? Well Android Studio's very helpful in pointing out we can set the color, the font size, the font weight, the font style, letter spacing. Let's start by changing the font size. I'm going to change it to a 40 point font. I'm going to hit save so we can see what it looks like. Yeah, that looks pretty good, size-wise. And then I'm going to change the color, I want it to be white. So let's write colors. The last thing I'm going to do is I'm going to make it bold. So I'm going to write *fontWeight* and I'm going to write *fontWeight.bold*. Now, let's hit save and you can see that we now have a bolded piece of text that's going to represent our name.

Now, the only difference between how it looks in our project and how we want it to ultimately look is that this is a different font. So, how can we incorporate our custom fonts into our projects, rather than just using the system default fonts?

5.7 Incorporating Custom Fonts in Your Flutter App

Flutter works with custom fonts and you can incorporate them to an individual widget or across an entire app. Having learned how to create a new application in Flutter, it's time to add custom fonts to your project.

With the following steps, you can easily create an app that uses custom fonts.

Import the font files – it is common to incorporate font files in the fonts or assets folder. This folder is found at the root of a Flutter project. What you need to do is to import the font files into the project. You can also download fonts from **Google Fonts** (www.fonts.google.com) and save them in the fonts folder. Just copy the downloaded fonts and paste them in the new assets directory.

In my example, I'm using four fonts" pacific regular, pacific bold, robotoCondensed regular, and robotoCondensed bold.

Register the fonts in the *pubspec.yaml* file. This is the code you'll need to configure the file in your *pubspec.yaml* file.

fonts:

   - family: Pacifico

      fonts:

         - asset: fonts/Pacifico-Regular.ttf

   - family: RobotoCondensed

      fonts:

         - asset: fonts/RobotoCondensed-Regular.ttf

         - asset: fonts/RobotoCondensed-Bold.ttf

            weight: 700

Go to the *main.dart* file and use the fonts to style your text. See the code below:

import 'package:Flutter/material.dart';

void main() => runApp(MyApp());

class MyApp extends StatelessWidget {

@override

Widget build(BuildContext context) {

   return MaterialApp(

      theme: ThemeData(

         primarySwatch: Colors.purple,

      ),

      home: MyHomePage(),

   );

```
  }
}

class MyHomePage extends StatefulWidget {
  @override
  _MyHomePageState createState() => _MyHomePageState();
}

class _MyHomePageState extends State<MyHomePage> {
  @override
  Widget build(BuildContext context) {
    return Scaffold(
      appBar: AppBar(
        title: Text('Flutter Custom Fonts'),
      ),
      body: Center(
        child: Column(
          mainAxisAlignment: MainAxisAlignment.center,
          children: <Widget>[
            Text(
              'Pacifico Regular',
              style: TextStyle(
```

```
          fontFamily: 'Pacifico', fontSize: 32.0, color:
Colors.purple),
      ),
      Text(
        'Pacifico Bold',
        style: TextStyle(
            fontFamily: 'Pacifico',
            fontWeight: FontWeight.bold,
            fontSize: 32.0,
            color: Colors.purple),
      ),
      Text(
        'RobotoCondensed Regular',
        style: TextStyle(
            fontFamily: 'RobotoCondensed', fontSize: 32.0, color:
Colors.purple),
      ),
      Text(
        'RobotoCondensed Bold',
        style: TextStyle(
            fontFamily: 'RobotoCondensed',
            fontWeight: FontWeight.w700,
            fontSize: 32.0,
            color: Colors.purple),
```

```
        ),
       ],
      ),
    ),
  );
}
}
```

Now, run the app and test it on the emulator, simulator or your device. Does the output look like the picture below?

Pacifico Regular

Pacifico Bold

RobotoCondensed Regular

RobotoCondensed Bold

5.8 Adding Material Icons With the Icon Widget

Material icons are those icons which you use in accordance to material design guidelines. They help make your app look more elegant. Let's look at how to add these icons in Flutter using the icon widget.

You can add an icon as seen below:

Icon(

  Icons.add,

color: Colors.pink,

size: 30.0,

)

Now, *add* is the icon name. There are several lists of material icons you can find on the web. The *color* feature is used to define the color of the icon while the *size* property determines the height and width of the icon.

The following code is an example of how to add a complete material icon.

import 'package:Flutter/material.dart';

void main() => runApp(MyApp());

class MyApp extends StatelessWidget {

@override

Widget build(BuildContext context) {

return MaterialApp(

title: 'Welcome to Flutter',

home: Scaffold(

appBar: AppBar(

title: Text('Flutter Material Icon Example'),

),

//calling MyBody class

body: Center(child:Icon(

Icons.verified_user,
color: Colors.teal,
size: 100.0,
),),
),
);
}
}

The output is this:

5.9 Flutter Card and ListTile Widget

Flutter Card and ListTile widgets are very flexible and are used most times with a list in Flutter. Fortunately, both of them are related. So, users can create a ListWidget using ListTile widget as its child.

ListTile is a widget that contains up to three lines of text by the sides of other widgets or icons like checkboxes. The first line of text is designated with the title and is mandatory. While the value of subtitle (which is not compulsory) will take the place allocated for an extra line of text, or even two lines provided, *ThreeLine* is true.

Oftentimes, the ListView widget requires a list of items and a good list is paramount for creating a simple looking card. This will not require you to specify the boundary.

Here comes the code:

ListView(

children: <Widget>[

ListTile()

],

),

Properties of ListTile Widget

ListTile Widget has the following properties:

title – This is the first line of the ListTile Widget and it takes up the top region and includes a Text widget as its value. You can create an easy ListTile Widget with the title feature as shown below:

ListView(

children: <Widget>[

ListTile(

title: Text("ListTile Title Example"),

)

],

),

Guess what the output would be? Run it in your device, emulator, or simulator!

> ListTile Title Example

subtitle – It takes up the second line of the ListTile Widget. The subtitle also includes the value of the Text Widget. This is the code:

ListTile(

title: Text("ListTile Title Example"),

subtitle: Text("ListTile Subtitle"),

)

The output? Try it!

> ListTile Title Example
> ListTile Subtitle

trailing – Here comes another attribute that includes an image or icon as its value. It occupies the flanks of the ListTile Widget and creates a simple list. The code for this description is:

ListTile(

title: Text("ListTile Title Example"),

subtitle: Text("ListTile Subtitle"),

trailing: Icon(Icons.add),

Can you figure out the output? Here you are!

> ListTile Title Example   +
> ListTile Subtitle

contentPadding – The contentPadding feature provides padding to the content within the ListTile Widget. Then, the title or subtitle is padded on all the flanks by the ListTile Widget. The code is straightforward.

ListTile(

title: Text("ListTile Title Example"),

subtitle: Text("ListTile Subtitle"),

trailing: Icon(Icons.add),

contentPadding: EdgeInsets.all(50.0),

)

The output is:

    ListTile Title Example   +
    ListTile Subtitle

dense - dense is a feature that lets the Flutter engine choose if the items should be arranged in vertical order or not. The distinction is that the Title and Subtitle difference is removed and all of the Text looks the same provided that dense is set to false.

This is the code:

ListTile(

title: Text("ListTile Title Example"),

subtitle: Text("ListTile Subtitle"),

trailing: Icon(Icons.add),

dense: false,

)

The output is this:

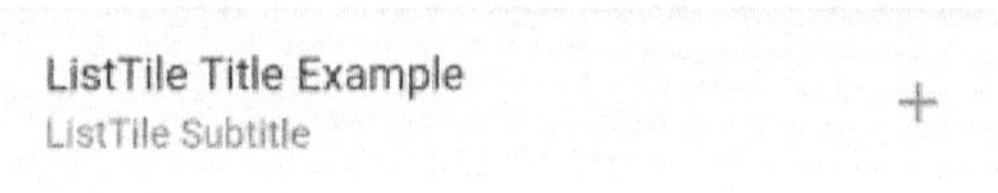

    ListTile Title Example   +
    ListTile Subtitle

isThreeLine - The ListTile is designed to show only two lines, the Title and the SubTitle, respectively. However, if there is a third line of text to be shown, the *isThreeLine* is set to true so it can allow another line to be added. The subtitle will be taking care of giving the 3rd line of text.

ListTile(

title: Text("ListTile Title Example"),

subtitle: Text("Sample Subtitle. \nSubtitle line 3"),

trailing: Icon(Icons.add),

isThreeLine: true,

)

Here comes the output:

ListTile Title Example
Sample Subtitle.
Subtitle line 3

leading - Leading is another feature that allows any widget to be included to the left of the Title and Subtitle widget. This part is given to the Leading feature. Just like the trailing widget which fills the space to the right of the Title or Subtitle, the leading fills the left flank. The code is written below:

ListTile(

title: Text("ListTile Title Example"),

subtitle: Text("Sample Subtitle. \nSubtitle line 3"),

trailing: Icon(Icons.add),

leading: Icon(Icons.add_box),

isThreeLine: true,

)

This is the output:

> ListTile Title Example
> Sample Subtitle.
> Subtitle line 3

onLongProcess() - To create the control for the LongPress on the ListTile Widget, the onLongPress callback is used. It gets started anytime the user clicks on the ListTile.

ListTile(

title: Text("ListTile Title Example"),

subtitle: Text("Sample Subtitle. \nSubtitle line 3"),

trailing: Icon(Icons.add),

leading: Icon(Icons.add_box),

isThreeLine: true,

onLongPress: () {

print("User Long Press Tile");

},

)

What do you think the output would be? *"User Long Press Tile"??*

onTap() - If there are actions to be performed when the user taps on the Title this callback can be used. Just like onLongPress, onTap is used when the user clicks on any item of the ListTile.

ListTile(

title: Text("ListTile Title Example"),

subtitle: Text("Sample Subtitle. \nSubtitle line 3"),

trailing: Icon(Icons.add),

leading: Icon(Icons.add_box),

isThreeLine: true,

onTap: () {

print("On Tap is Clicked");

},

)

What is the output? Try it out and see!

Chapter 5 Tip – Hard Things Are Worth Doing

These are the properties that are included in Row and Column widgets. The aim of this chapter has been to provide you with an insight on how to build beautiful user interfaces using Flutter widgets, as well as a short description of the Row and Column widget in Flutter. Now, it's time to apply these ideas and get more familiar with them. Remember that practice makes perfect. Apply these skills yourself and see where you need improvement.

Chapter Summary

- By now, you should know what it takes to create beautiful and elegant user interfaces from Flutter widgets. From Flutter Layout Challenge to how to perform hot reload in your app and how to use container widgets, I hope you found this chapter fun.
- Now, it is time to turn to chapter 6 and see what it has in store for us. Be ready to explore how to build apps.

Chapter Six: Building Apps with State

As you discover more and more options in Flutter, a time will come when you'll need to share application states between screens and across your application. There are many ways to do that as well as certain steps to take to achieve that. The lessons that follow talk about the basics of handling state in Flutter app.

It's time to learn state management techniques in Flutter that are used to manage information stored in the application's memory, like active user interface elements, notifications, user preferences, and other data. There are many different ways to manage state and this chapter introduces you to the fundamentals.

Here, you'll learn how to create changeable layouts, use functions to shape and improve your code, add variables and data types, as well as leverage stateful and stateless widgets.

6.1 A stateful dice app (Dice Project)

Here, I will tell you how to make a dice roller app using Flutter. The first step is to download six (6) dice images from: https://github.com/itsmebrp/Flutter_diceroller. Attach those six images you downloaded for each dice side. Create an image folder in the project directory and move those files in there. In this case, the image folder is named img. Here's the code for adding those image files to pubspec.yaml.

assets:

    - img/

\#   - images/a_dot_ham.jpeg

Having added these images to assets and saved them, it's time to move to main.dart and start coding.

Now, you will create a new file called home_page.dart by creating the main function and adding a stateless widget. Here's a screenshot of the code:

```dart
import 'package:dice_roller/home_page.dart';
import 'package:flutter/material.dart';

void main()=> runApp(BRPApp());

class BRPApp extends StatelessWidget {
  @override
  Widget build(BuildContext context) {
    return MaterialApp(
      title: "Dice Roller App",
      debugShowCheckedModeBanner: false,
      theme: ThemeData.dark(),
      home: HomePage()
    ); // MaterialApp
  }
}
```

The next step is to open the home_page.dart and create a stateful widget called HomePage. The screenshot of the code is:

```dart
import 'dart:math';
import 'package:flutter/material.dart';

class HomePage extends StatefulWidget {
  @override
  _HomePageState createState() => _HomePageState();
}
class _HomePageState extends State<HomePage> {
  AssetImage one = AssetImage("img/1.png");
  AssetImage two = AssetImage("img/2.png");
  AssetImage three = AssetImage("img/3.png");
  AssetImage four = AssetImage("img/4.png");
  AssetImage five = AssetImage("img/5.png");
  AssetImage six = AssetImage("img/6.png");
  int diceimage;
  @override
  void initState() {
    super.initState();

    setState(() {
      diceimage = 1;
    });
  }

  void rollDice() {
    int ranrom = (Random().nextInt(6)) + 1;
    setState(() {
      diceimage = ranrom;
      print(diceimage);
    });
  }
```

```dart
27        int ranrom = (Random().nextInt(6)) + 1;
28        setState(() {
29          diceimage = ranrom;
30          print(diceimage);
31        });
32      }
33
34      @override
35      Widget build(BuildContext context) {
36        return Scaffold(
37          appBar: AppBar(
38            title: Text('Dice Roller Game'),
39          ), // AppBar
40          body: Container(
41            child: Center(
42              child: Column(
43                mainAxisAlignment: MainAxisAlignment.center,
44                children: <Widget>[
45                  Image.asset(
46                    "img/$diceimage.png",
47                    width: 200,
48                    height: 200,
49                  ), // Image.asset
50                  Container(
51                    width: MediaQuery.of(context).size.width * 0.8,
52                    margin: EdgeInsets.only(top: 100),
53                    child: ClipRRect(
54                      borderRadius: BorderRadius.circular(10),
55                      child: FlatButton(
56                        child: Text('Press Me'),
57                        color: Colors.indigo,
```

```
              child: ClipRRect(
                borderRadius: BorderRadius.circular(10),
                child: FlatButton(
                  child: Text('Press Me'),
                  color: Colors.indigo,
                  padding:
                      EdgeInsets.symmetric(vertical: 20, horizontal: 40),
                  onPressed: () => rollDice()), // FlatButton
              ), // ClipRRect
            ), // Container
            SizedBox(
              height: 10,
            ), // SizedBox
            Text('Developed by: Bishworaj Poudel')
          ], // <Widget>[]
        ), // Column
      ), // Center
    ), // Container
  ); // Scaffold
  }
}
```

After writing this long lists of code, run the app. The output should look like this:

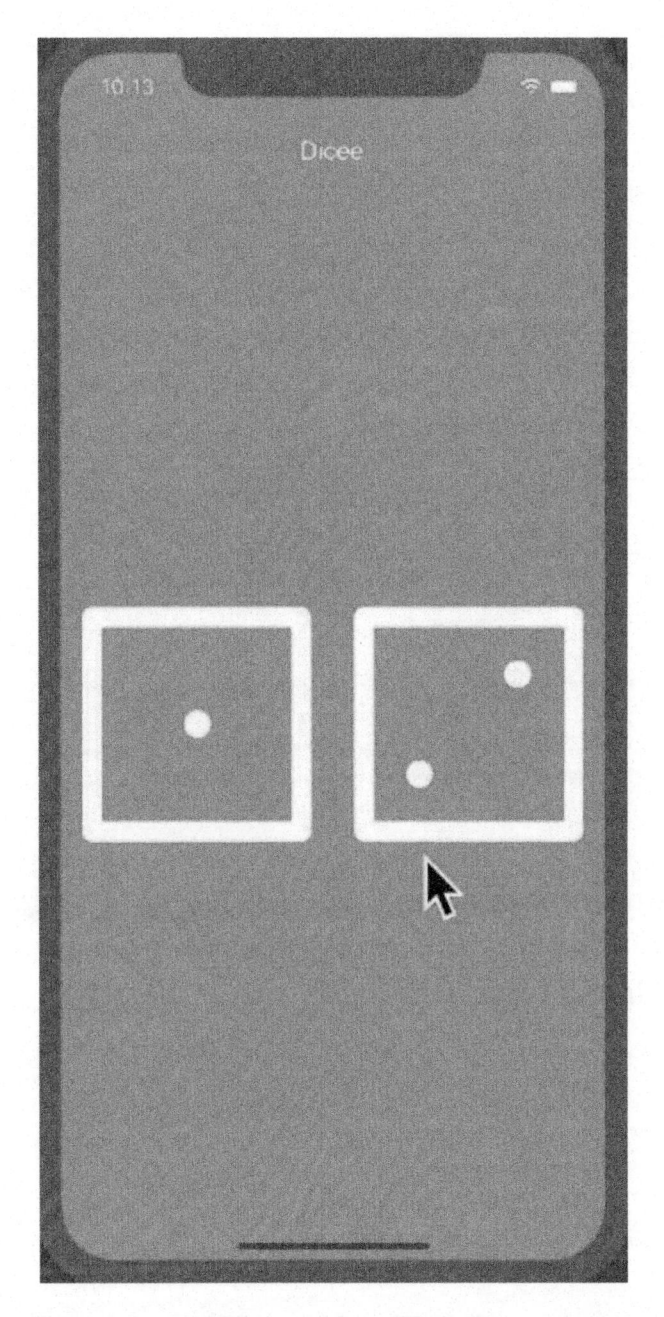

6.2 Using the Expanded Widget for Flexible Layouts

An expanded widget is tightly coupled with column, or row, or base flex widget as it can change the wild widget along the main axis of the parent column or row widget. The main axis is vertical for the column widget and horizontal for the row widget, whereas the cross axis dimension is not altered by the expanded widget.

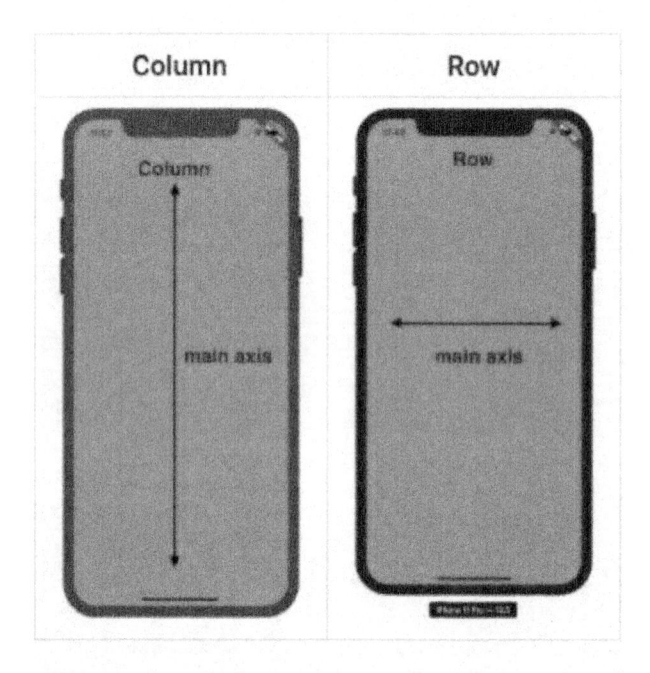

The essence of using expanded widgets is for the Flutter app to change and adapt to the screen size – responsive design. It is important for responsiveness as you cannot specify the size as a percentage of the screen.

For instance, the following responsive issue is easily solved by using expanded widget.

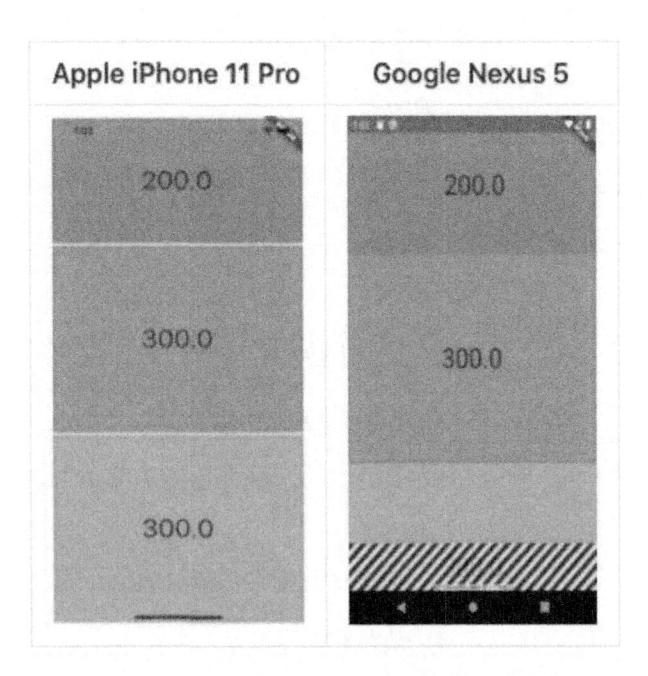

Apple iPhone 11 Pro	Google Nexus 5
200.0 / 300.0 / 300.0	200.0 / 300.0

Now, using an expanded widget means that you use a flexible widget with tight fit. Here's the code:

Widget build(BuildContext context) {

　　return Scaffold (

　　　　body: Column(

　　　　mainAxisAlignment: MainAxisAlignment.spaceBetween,

　　　　　　children: <Widget>[

　　　　　　　　Container (

　　　　　　　　　　color: Colors.lightBlue

　　　　　　　　　　height: 600,

　　　　　　　　　　width: double.infinity,

　　　　　　　　　　child: Center (

```
                    child: Text(
                    '600.0',
                    style: TextStyle (fontsize: 40.0),
                ))),
                Expanded (,
                  child: Container (,
                    color: Colors.green,
                    height: 80, // HEIGHT IGNORED BY EXPANDED
                    width: double.infinity,
                    child: Center (
                    child: Text (
                      'Expanded – shorthand for flexible with tight fit',
                      style: TextStyle (fontSize: 25.0),
                ))),
              ),
            ],
          ),
        );
    }
```

The output is shown below:

So, if you want a widget to expand as much to the available space there is along the main axis with a column or row, use the expanded widget as shown.

6.3 How to Use Intention Actions

As you code in your Flutter main.dart page, your Flutter editor analyzes your code, looks for ways to optimize it, and locates potential and actual problems and fixes them.

Once the integrated development environment (IDE) finds a way to change your code, it shows a yellow bulb icon in your editor next to the current line. If you click on the icon, you can see **intention actions** available for this particular line of code.

Intention actions include a wide range of conditions ranging from warnings to optimization advice and suggestions. You can see the complete list of intentions as well as customize them in the Settings/Preferences dialog or by pressing Alt+Ctrl+S in your keyboard.

A red bulb with an exclamation sign shows that your Flutter editor has detected an issue and requires you to choose an associated solution, which is a quick fix. Now, the combination of quick fixes and intention actions is called context actions.

How to use intention actions in Flutter

Click on the bulb icon or press Alt + Enter from the keyboard to see the list of suggestions and choose an action from the list. More so, some intention actions require that you open a preview by pressing Shift+Ctrl+I or click "view/quick definition".

For instance, your Flutter editor provides an idea that converts *.format()* calls and *printf* style formatting to *f-string* words.

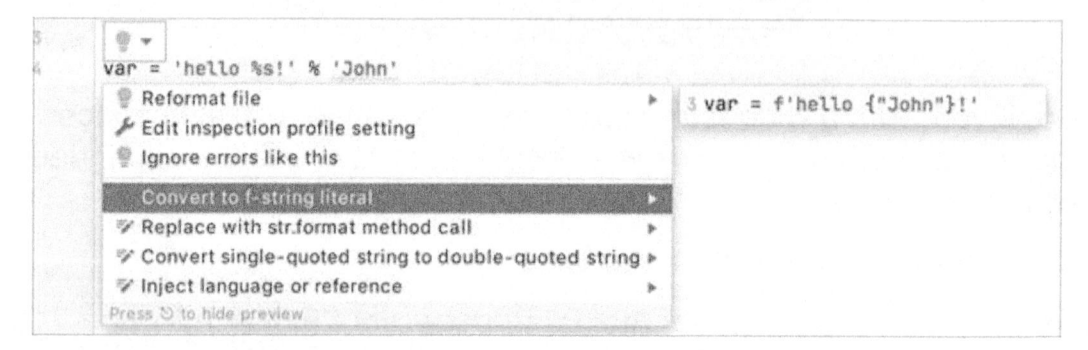

Press the enter key to apply the selected intention and you'll have the following output:

```
3
4       var = f'hello {"John"}!'
```

The way *f-string* words show on the editor depends on the nature of color settings. In the settings/preference dialog (Ctrl+Alt+S), you can change the available settings by navigating to editor/color scheme/python and choosing *string/f-string* in the lists of components there. Also, this is where you can view the complete list of available intention actions and disable the ones you don't need.

Select editor/intentions from the settings/preferences dialog, for every intention action, you will see an overview and an example. Just clear the checkbox next to it, to disable the intention. Apply the changes and close the dialog box. That's all!

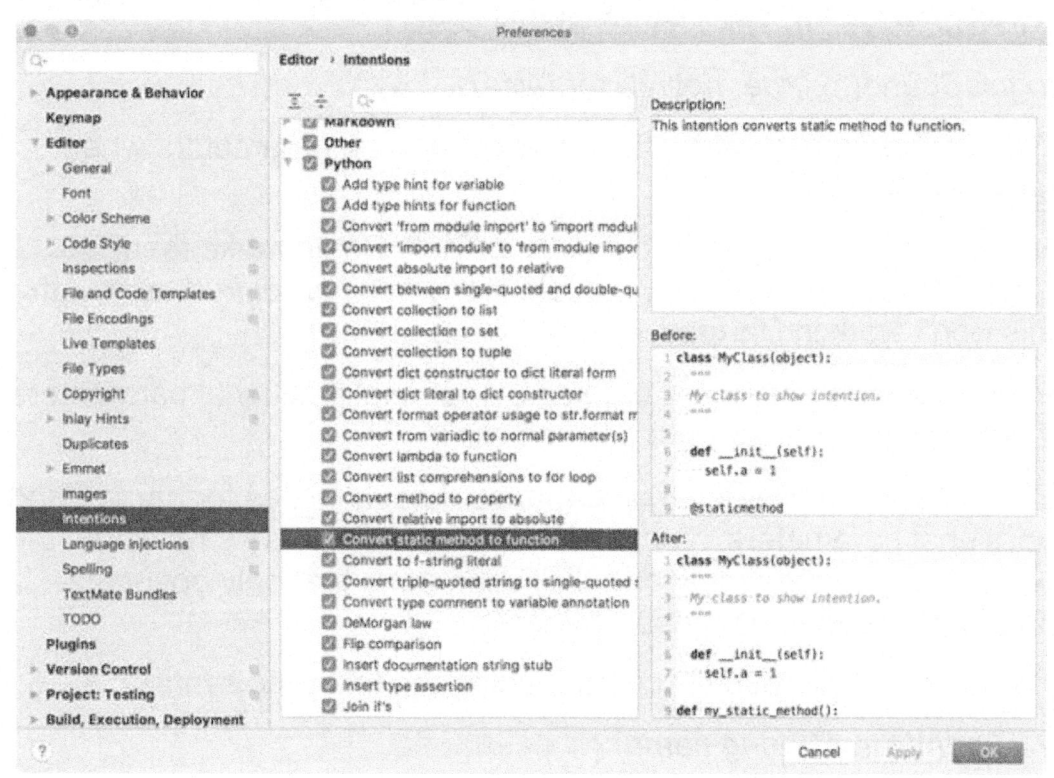

177

6.4 Dart Functions Part

In this tutorial, we're going to discuss functions in dart and how they work. Functions are objects in dart that can be assigned to variables and passed to other functions. They are also blocks of code that perform a single task. They are organized, reusable, and related to the class under consideration.

Function Parameters

Dart Functions can have two types of parameters such as **required** and **optional** parameters. The **required** parameters take the front row, then the **optional** ones follow suit. However, **optional** parameters can be **named** or **positional** but not both parameters.

How to use parameters

We can specify named parameters when calling a function by using *paraName: value*. Take a look at this code:

toggleSound(to: true, notifyUser:false);

We use the *{para1, para2, ...}* to show named parameters when defining a function.

Named parameters are optional by default. So, to make them required, we have to briefly explain them with *@required*, although this won't work in Dartpad.

Positional parameters are marked as optional positional parameters if we wrap a set of function parameters in [ ].

We can set compile-time constants as default values for named and positional parameters, respectively. However, if there's no value, the parameters will be empty or null. That means that only optional parameters can have default values.

The functions are usually created using the following syntax:

void printName(String name) {

print(name)

    }

Where

- **void** is the return type of function. It means that when the function runs all the code inside, it should return this value. But in this case, we're not returning anything. Rather, we're printing a name because we don't need to return a value.
- **printName** is the name of the function. It explains what this function is.
- **String name** (in parenthesis) specify the type of parameter and the name of that parameter.

For example,

Integer sum(Integer a, Integer b) {

    return a+b;

}

The above function helps add two integers; we provide the first and second value, and it returns the sum of both.

The void main() function

The void main() function serves the mandatory role of linking every app we build with an entry point. Then, the function returns void and possesses the optional list<string> parameter for arguments.

Recursive Functions – Recursion is a strategy that is used for repeating an operation by having a function call to itself iteratively until it produces an outcome. It is best used when you want to call the same function repeatedly with diverse parameters in a loop. The example of the code below produces a result or an output of 720.

void main() {

```
    print(factorial(6));
}
factorial(number) {
   if (number <= 0) {
       // termination case
       return 1;
   } else {
       return (number * factorial(number - 1));
       // function invokes itself
   }
}
```

Lambda Functions – These are a short strategy to represent functions. They're also called arrow functions. Syntax is: *[return_type]function_name(parameters)=>expression;*

Here's an example:

```
void main() {
   printMsg();
   print(test());
}
printMsg()=>
print("hello");


int test()=>123;
```

// returning function

The output is: hello 123.

Functions are the cornerstone of managing program complexity and are objects in Dart.

6.5 Dart Variables

Variables in Dart are used to store the value and refer the memory location in computer memory that holds a value for that variable. When we create a variable, the Dart compiler allocates some space in the memory. The size of the memory block of memory is based on the type of variable. Here is an example of a creating variable and assigning value to it.

var name = 'Dansaki';

Rules for Creating a Variable in dart

Creating a variable with the right name is an important assignment in any programming language. To create a variable, certain rules are adhered to. The Dart has some rules to define a variable. These rules are below:

- The variable cannot contain special characters such as whitespace, mathematical symbol, runes, Unicode character, and keywords.
- The first character of the variable should be an alphabet([A to Z],[a to z]). Digits cannot be the first character.
- Variables are case sensitive. For instance, the variable 'angel' and ANGEL' are treated differently, as they are important.
- Variable names can be made up of letters and alphabets.
- Characters like #, @, ^, &, * are not permitted as they're special. The only characters allowed are underscore(_) and the dollar sign($).
- Blank spaces are not permitted in a variable name.

- The variable name should be readable and related to the program.

How to Declare Variables

When using a variable, it is important that we declare it before using it in a program. The **var** keyword is used to declare a variable in Dart. The Dart compiler automatically knows the type of data based on the value assigned to the variable as Dart is an infer type language. The syntax is given in either of the two statements below.

var <variable_name> = <value>;

var <variable_name>;

for instance,

var name = 'Station'

In the above example, the variable **name** has allocated some space in the memory. The semicolon(;) is important to use as it separates program statements from one another.

Annotations in Dart

Dart is an infer language but it also provides a type annotation. While declaring the variable, it suggests the type of the value that the variable can store. In the type annotation, we add the data type as a prefix before the variable's name that ensures that the variable can store specific data type. The syntax is given below.

<type> <variable_name>; or

<type> <name> = <expression>;

Here comes an example:

int figure;

String msg = "The day is bright";

In the above example, we have declared a variable named **figure** which will store the integer data. The variable named **msg** stored the string type data.

How to Declare Multiple Variables

Dart offers a way of declaring multiple values of the same type to the variables. We can do this in a single statement, and each value is separated by a comma. The syntax is given below.

<type> <var1,var2....varN>;

The following is an example:

int a, b, c;

Assigning of a Variable in Dart

The usual equal sign (=) is used in Dart to assign values to a variable. It is called the assignment operator. The operand on the left side of the assignment operator shows the name of the variable while the operand on the right side of the assignment operator shows the value to be included in the variable.

For instance, the following code shows an example of assignment statement:

Int ctr;

Ctr = 7; // Assignment Statement

In a single statement, it is possible to assign and declare an initial value to a variable. The syntax for this purpose is:

<type> <name> = <expression>;

An example code is this: *int counter = 5;*

Declaring Default Value

While declaring the variable without initializing the value, the Dart compiler provides a default value (Null) to the variable. Even the numeric type variables are initially assigned with the null value. Take a look at the example below.

int count;

assert(count == null);

Using Final and Const

Now, if you don't want to change a variable in the future, then use final and const. It can be used in place of **var** or in addition to a type. A final variable can be set only once when the variable is a compile-time constant. The example of creating a final variable is given below.

final name = 'Urchman';   // final variable without type annotation.

final String msg = 'Are you there?'; //final variable with type annotation.

If you try to change these values, an error will occur.

name = 'Davis';   // Error: Final variable can't be changed.

The const is used to create compile-time constants. You can even declare a value to compile-time constant like number, string literal, a const variable, etc.

const z = 100;

The const keyword is also used to create a constant value that cannot be changed after its creation.

var = const[];

If you try to change it, an error will take place.

f = [14];   //Error, The const variable cannot be changed

6.6 Dart Data Types

Data types are the most important basic features of a programming language. In Dart, the data type of the variable is defined by its value. The main function of variables is that they're used to hold values and reserve a memory location. The data type describes the type of value that will be stored by the variable. Every variable has its data type. The Dart is a static type of language in the sense that the variables cannot change.

There are six basic types of Data available in Dart. So, in this section, we will learn all the data types available in Dart and look at examples.

Dart Number - The Dart number is used to hold the numeric values. The number is made up of two types namely, integer and double.

- Integer - Integer value represents the whole number or non-fractional values. An integer data type shows the 64-bit non-decimal numbers ranging from -263 to 263. A variable can store an unsigned or signed integer value. Here's an example:

int marks = 20;

- Double - Double value represents the 64-bit of information (double-precision) for a floating number or numbers with large decimal points. The double keyword is used to declare the double type variable. For instance:

double pi = 3.14;

Dart Strings – In Dart, a string is defined as the sequence of the character. If we store the data such as name, address, special character, and others; It is signified by using either a single quote or double quotes. A Dart string is an ordered series of UTF-16 code units.

var msg = "Welcome to My World";

Or

String name1 = 'Code';

String name2 = "Write";

print(name1 + ' ' +name2);

Output should read Code Write.

Dart Boolean - The Boolean type represents the two values - true and false. The 'bool' keyword is used to show Boolean Type and during declaration time. The numeric values 1 and 0 cannot be used to represent the true or false value. Here is an example:

bool isValid = true;

Or

bool val1 = true;

bool val2 = false;

print(val1);

print (val2);

The output should be true and false

Dart lists - In Dart, **List** is a collection of the ordered objects (value). The elements in the list are separated by the comma wrapped in a square bracket[]. An example list is provided below.

var list = [1,2,3] or

List<int> rollNum = List(3);

  rollNum[0] = 2;

  rollNum[1] = 3;

  rollNum[2] = 4;

  for (int elements in rollNum) {

print(elements);

}

The output should be the following: 2, 3, 4.

Dart Maps - The map type is used to store values in key-value pairs. Each key is associated with its value. The key and value can be any type. In a Dart Map, the key must be unique, but a value can occur multiple times. The Map is defined by using curly braces ({}) and a comma separates each pair. For instance:

var student = {'name': 'Jude', 'age':18, 'Branch': 'Social Science'}

Dart Runes – Strings are the sequence of Unicode UTF-16 code units. *What is Unicode then?*

It is a code which is used to represent a special numeric value for each digit, letter, and symbol. Since Dart Runes are unique strings of Unicode UTF-32 units, they are used to describe special syntax.

For instance: The unique heart character ♥ is equivalent to Unicode code \u2665, where \u means Unicode, and the numbers are hexadecimal integers. If the hex value is less or greater than 4 digits, it goes in a curly bracket ({}).

Chapter 6 Tip – How to Deal with Procrastination

We've just gone over the basics when it comes to building apps with state. To get a hold of all things involved here, practice is a necessity. These ideas would become simpler if you handle some projects on your own. This will help you get the feel of how the app responds to state.

If you are wondering why we couldn't take out the Expanded widget and the repeated FlatButton widget or the repeated onPressed on the challenge in section 6.13, we're going to answer that in the modules ahead. Besides, we need to learn more about widgets before we can do that.

Chapter Summary

State management techniques discussed in chapter 6 helped us learn how to manage data stored in an application's memory such as active UI elements, etc. We took time to study the following:

- How to use functions to control and boost your code.
- How to add data and variables.
- Data types.
- Stateful and stateless widgets.
- Different challenges and many more

I've got one big challenge for you, and it's to **build an app of your own**. Try to implement all that we've studied so far and you cannot fail!

Chapter Seven: Deploying Gesture and User Input

Flutter can define new custom user interface elements using Dart code. This is one of the most surprising things about Flutter which no other cross-platform app development instrument can do.

In this chapter, I will show you how simple it is to develop your custom user interface elements from the start, so that you'll have the ability to customize the look of your app. Besides, you'll no longer battle with the built-in components of your device because you don't depend on third party libraries anymore.

7.1 Stateful Versus Stateless Widgets

With reference to our intro about stateful and stateless widgets in section 6.4 of this chapter, it is clear this concept is no longer new to you.

In Flutter, every user interface component is known as widget. The widget contains the code for a single screen of the app and it can be of two types, stateful and stateless.

Stateless Widgets are those widgets whose state cannot be changed (immutable) once they're built. Simply put, stateless widgets cannot modify their state when the app is being run. Thus, you cannot redraw the widgets when the app is in action. Below is the fundamental structure of a stateless widget:

import 'package:Flutter/material.dart';

void main() => runApp(MyApp());

class MyApp extends StatelessWidget {

  @override

  Widget build(BuildContext context) {

    return Container();

  }

}

The name of the stateless widget above is *MyApp*. It is called from the *runApp()* and extends the widget. Within the *MyApp*, a build function is taken control of and *BuildContext* becomes a parameter. The *BuildContext* is unique to each widget because it is used to find the widget within the widget tree.

Some examples of stateless widgets are text, icon, and chip. You can create a stateless widget in Android Studio or VS Code by applying the shortcut 'stl'.

Stateful Widgets are those widgets whose state can be changed even multiple times once they're built. This means that the state of an app can be altered many times with different sets of data, variables, etc.

The basic structure of a stateful widget is shown below:

```
import 'package:Flutter/material.dart';
void main() => runApp(MyApp());
class MyApp extends StatefulWidget {
  @override
  _MyAppState createState() => _MyAppState();
}


class _MyAppState extends State<MyApp> {
  @override
  Widget build(BuildContext context) {
    return Container();
  }
}
```

Looking at the code above, *MyApp* is the name of the stateful widget which is being called from the *runApp()* and extends a stateful widget. Within the *MyAPP* class, we take control of the create state function. Then, the *createState()* function is used to build a changeable state for this widget at a particular location in the widget tree.

This approach returns an instance for the state subclass. The other class, *_MyAppState,* extends the state, which controls all the changes in the widget. Within this class, the build function is taken control of, which takes the *BuildContext* as the parameter.

The build function returns the widget where we build the user interface of the app. You can call the build function multiple times to create the whole user interface once more to incorporate all the changes, since it is a stateful widget.

Some examples of stateful widgets are radio, textfield, and checkbox. You can build a stateful widget in Android Studio or VS Code by implementing the shortcut 'stf'.

7.2 Detecting User Interaction With Flutter Buttons

Having gone this far in our coding trainings, let's see if you can create the following layouts by yourself:

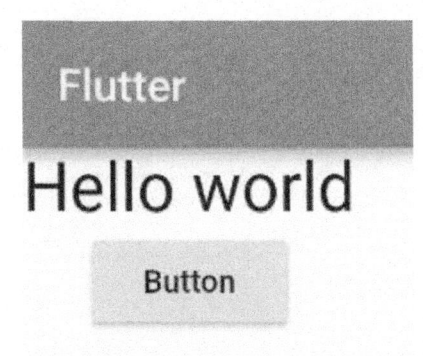

How did you do? Were you able to do it? If you weren't able to perform such a simple programming exercise, then, I suggest that you refer back to our previous chapters on layouts. If you succeeded, then your code probably looks like this:

void main() => runApp(MyApp());

      class MyApp extends StatelessWidget { //   <-- *StatelessWidget*

    @override

    Widget build(BuildContext context) {

    return MaterialApp(

    ...

```
body: myLayoutWidget(),
...
}

Widget myLayoutWidget() {
return Column(
children: [
Text(...),
RaisedButton(...),
],
);
}
```

The layout above works well. However, if you modify the text when the button is pressed, you're likely to have issues.. This is because widgets are unchangeable, but they can only be recreated. To recreate the Text widget, you need to put the string into a variable. That variable is called the state, which refers to the values (current conditions) of the variables attached to that widget.

The code above is a *StatelessWidget* as it doesn't have any state. This means it doesn't have any changeable variable. But if you have any value you want to change, then you need a *StatefulWidget*.

StatefulWidgets have the following features:
- They have a StatefulWidget class as well as a state class.
- The StatefulWidget class sets the state class and gets it ready.
- The state class supports the variable and informs the StatefulWidget class when and how to develop itself.

So, whenever you want to build a StatefulWidget, you need to create two classes namely, widget class and a state class. The basic code looks like this:

// widget class

```
class MyWidget extends StatefulWidget {
@override
_MyWidgetState createState() => _MyWidgetState();
}


// state class
class _MyWidgetState extends State<MyWidget> {
@override
Widget build(BuildContext context) {
return ...; // widget layout
}
}
```

Two important points to note here:

- The widget class has a *createState()* feature that returns the State. The State class has a *build()* feature that builds the widget.
- Also, the _ *underscore* at the start of the name *_MyWidgetState* makes it private. It can only be seen in this file. This is a feature of the Dart language.

Understanding the concept of state will help you get ready to make the widgets respond to user input. Among the responsive widgets we'll use are buttons. Let's do a bit of coding right now.

Open your *main.dart* file and write the following code:

import 'package:Flutter/material.dart';

void main() => runApp(MyApp());

```
// boilerplate code
class MyApp extends StatelessWidget {
@override
Widget build(BuildContext context) {
return MaterialApp(
title: 'Flutter',
home: Scaffold(
appBar: AppBar(
    title: Text('Flutter'),
),
body: MyWidget(),
),
);
}
}

// widget class
class MyWidget extends StatefulWidget {
```

```
  @override
  _MyWidgetState createState() => _MyWidgetState();
}


  // state class
  // We will replace this class in each of the examples below
  class _MyWidgetState extends State<MyWidget> {

  // state variable
  String _textString = 'Hello world';


  // The State class will incorporate this method, which creates the widget
  @override
  Widget build(BuildContext context) {
    return Column(
      children: [
        Text(
          _textString,
          style: TextStyle(fontSize: 30),
        ),
        RaisedButton( //                    <--- Button
          child: Text('Button'),
          onPressed: () {
```

```
          _doSomething();
        },
      ),
    ],
  );
}


  // this private method is run whenever the button is pressed
  void _doSomething() {
    // Using the callback State.setState() is the only way to get the build
    // method to rerun with the updated state value.
    setState(() {
      _textString = 'Hello Flutter';
    });
  }
}
```

Now, run the code. You'll notice that it looks like the original layout but now, if you press the button for the first time, the text is updated.

Take note of the following points:

- The *RaisedButton* widget has an *onPressed* parameter where you can add a function that will be called whenever the button is pressed.
- You have to update variables inside the *setState()* feature if you want the changes to appear in the user interface.
- Perform a hot restart rather than a hot reload to bring back the state to the initial values.

TextFields – Anytime a TextField is modified, the Text widget is updated. Now, go to the code above and replace the *_MyWidgetState()* class with the following code:

class _MyWidgetState extends State<MyWidget> {

    String _textString = 'Hello world';

    @override
    Widget build(BuildContext context) {
    return Column(
    children: [
   Text(
      _textString,
      style: TextStyle(fontSize: 30),
),
   TextField(//   *<--- TextField*
      onChanged: (text) {
      _doSomething(text);
        },

```
      )
    ],
  );
}


    void _doSomething(String text) {
    setState(() {
    _textString = text;
    });
    }
      }
```

You'll notice that *TextField* has an *onChanged* parameter for a callback feature. This feature provides the current string after a change has been effected. Besides, the Text value can be gotten without even listening to *onChanged* and you can set the control parameter of the *TextField*.

Checkboxes – With a checkbox having a label as shown below, you can use the CheckboxListTile:

The following code will do the magic:

```
class _MyWidgetState extends State<MyWidget> {

    bool _checkedValue = false;
```

```dart
@override
Widget build(BuildContext context) {
  return CheckboxListTile( //                    <---CheckboxListTile
    title: Text('this is my title'),
    value: _checkedValue,
    onChanged: (newValue) {
      _doSomething(newValue);
    },
    // setting the controlAffinity to leading makes the checkbox come
    // before the title instead of after it
    controlAffinity: ListTileControlAffinity.leading,
  );
}

void _doSomething(bool isChecked) {
  setState(() {
    _checkedValue = isChecked;
  });
}
    }
```

The Checkbox widget does not have a title included in it. You can use it to create a custom checkbox.

Dialogues – There are only a few types of dialogues in Flutter, but AlertDialog is one of the commonest ones that is easy to set up. The following code produces the output you're seeing.

```
class _MyWidgetState extends State<MyWidget> {

  @override
  Widget build(BuildContext context) {
    return RaisedButton(
      child: Text('Button'),
      onPressed: () {
        _showAlertDialog();
      },
    );
  }

  void _showAlertDialog() {

    // set up the button
    Widget okButton = FlatButton(
      child: Text("OK"),
      onPressed: () {
```

```
        // This closes the dialog. `context` means the BuildContext, which is
        // available by default inside of a State object. If you are working
        // with an AlertDialog in a StatelessWidget, then you would need to
        // pass a reference to the BuildContext.
        Navigator.pop(context);
      },
    );

    // set up the AlertDialog
    AlertDialog alert = AlertDialog(
      title: Text("Dialog title"),
      content: Text("This is a Flutter AlertDialog."),
      actions: [
        okButton,
      ],
    );

    // show the dialog
    showDialog(
      context: context,
      builder: (BuildContext context) {
```

return alert;
  },
);

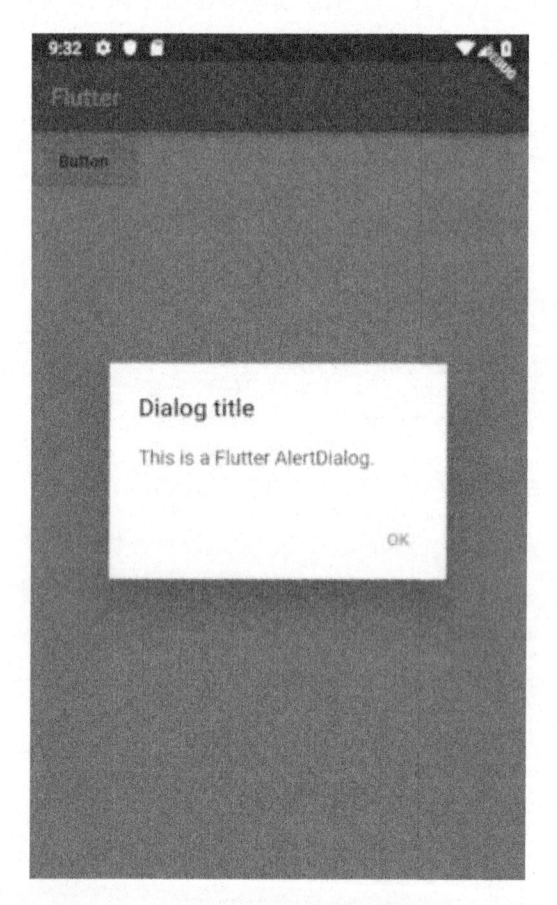

}
  }

Note that an AlertDialog requires the *BuildContext* feature which is passed into the *build()* feature and it is a property of the state object. Then, you close the dialog with the navigator.

From the examples shown above, you witnessed how user inputs interacted with some common widgets available. The widgets provide callback parameters such as *onPressed* and *onChanged*. However, other widgets such as *Container* or *Text* don't have a built-in way of interacting with them.

Gesture Detectors – Flutter provides an easy way to make the widgets we used above very interactive. All you have to do is to wrap any widget with a GestureDetector and you're good to go.

For instance, the following Text widget is wrapped with a GestureDetector widget.

GestureDetector(

    child: Text('Hello world'),

    onTap: () {

    // do something

    },

      );

When you tap the text, the onTap callback will be run. Everytime you tap the text, the color changes.

Here, the following code will produce the output below when you run it:

class _MyWidgetState extends State<MyWidget> {

    Color textColor = Colors.black;

    @override

```
Widget build(BuildContext context) {
return GestureDetector(  //            <--- GestureDetector
 child: Text(
  'Hello world',
  style: TextStyle(
        fontSize: 30,
        color: textColor,
  ),
 ),
 onTap: () { //                        <--- onTap
  _doSomething();
 },
);
}

void _doSomething() {
 setState(() {
  // have to import 'dart:math' in order to use Random()
  int randomHexColor = Random().nextInt(0xFFFFFF);
  int opaqueColor = 0xFF000000 + randomHexColor;
  textColor = Color(opaqueColor);
 });
}
```

}

> **Flutter**
> Hello world

There are a lot of gestures that are very easy to detect. All you have to do is to replace *onTap* in the code above with anyone of them. The following is how gestures are detected and you can play around with them to see what they do.

- onDoubleTap
- onLongPress
- onLongPressUp
- onPanDown
- onPanStart
- onPanUpdate
- onPanEnd
- onPanCancel
- onScaleStart
- onScaleUpdate
- onScaleEnd
- onTap
- onTapDown
- onTapUp
- onTapCancel
- onHorizontalDragDown
- onHorizontalDragUpdate
- onHorizontalDragEnd
- onHorizontalDragCancel
- onVerticalDragStart
- onVerticalDragDown
- onVerticalDragUpdate
- onVerticalDragEnd
- onVerticalDragCancel

Navigation – This deals with how you navigate to different screens in Flutter and return back. A new screen in Flutter represents a new widget and the ways to get to these widgets are called routes. So, Flutter uses a navigator to control the routes.

To display a new screen, you deploy the navigator to push a route to a stack. To close a screen and return to the previous screen, you move the route away from the top of the stack.

If you want to navigate to a new widget called *SecondScreen*, use the following code:

Navigator.push(

    context,

    MaterialPageRoute(

  builder: (context) => SecondScreen(),

    ));

The context is the *BuildContext* of the current widget that wants to navigate to the screen. The *MaterialPageRoute* creates the route to the new screen, while navigator.push indicates that we're adding the route to the stack.

If you want to return to the first screen from *SecondScreen*, use the following code:

Navigator.pop(context);

Do you remember we used this code to end the *AlertDialog* we made before?

Now run the following code:

import 'package:Flutter/material.dart';

    void main() {

```
runApp(MaterialApp(
title: 'Flutter',
home: FirstScreen(),
));
    }


    class FirstScreen extends StatelessWidget {
@override
    Widget build(BuildContext context) {
return Scaffold(
appBar: AppBar(title: Text('First screen')),
body: Center(
child: RaisedButton(
      child: Text(
      'Go to second screen',
        style: TextStyle(fontSize: 24),
      ),
      onPressed: () {
      _navigateToSecondScreen(context);
        },
)
),
);
```

```
}


void _navigateToSecondScreen(BuildContext context) {
  Navigator.push(
   context,
   MaterialPageRoute(
      builder: (context) => SecondScreen(),
  ));
}
    }


    class SecondScreen extends StatelessWidget {
@override
Widget build(BuildContext context) {
return Scaffold(
 appBar: AppBar(title: Text('Second screen')),
 body: Center(
  child: RaisedButton(
      child: Text(
      'Go back to first screen',
      style: TextStyle(fontSize: 24),
      ),
      onPressed: () {
```

```
            _goBackToFirstScreen(context);
          },
      ),
    ),
  );
}


void _goBackToFirstScreen(BuildContext context) {
    Navigator.pop(context);
}
    }
```
In the iOS simulator, the above code looks like this:

Chapter 7 Tip - Coding

As the taste of a pudding is in the eating, we'll now test our coding skills of what we've learned so far to see whether it really works. Don't give up, keep on practicing, keep on coding!

Chapter Summary

- This chapter has discussed stateless and stateful widgets as well as how most applications use some form of user interaction with the system. The number one step in creating an interactive application is to discover input gestures.

- In the next chapter, we'll dive into dice image challenges, where we'll get our brains and fingers very busy with some exercises.

Chapter Eight: Dice Image Challenges

There are different ways for managing state in Flutter. Here, you'll discover how to create more flexible layouts, deploy functions to improve your code, add variables and data types, and leverage Stateful and Stateless widgets. You'll have some challenges to test your new skills.

8.1 Making the Dice Image Change Reactively

In a previous chapter, specifically in section 6.1, we learned how we can wrap our images in a flat button so that when we click on the button, something happens. When you build an app in that way, it would not be too good as the user might not see what is happening.

So, we need to update our images based on when the user presses the button. This will make it an app with functionality.

We're going to create a variable inside our stateless widget. You can do this by using the keyword 'var' and giving it a name, say 'leftdicenumber'. This will refer to the number of the die that will be displayed on the left. See the snapshot of the code below:

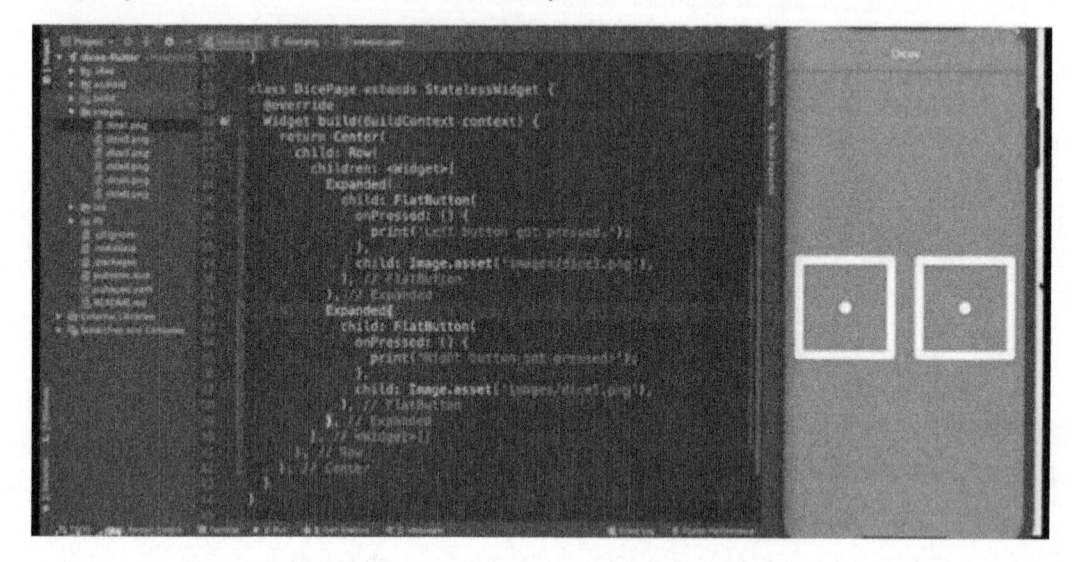

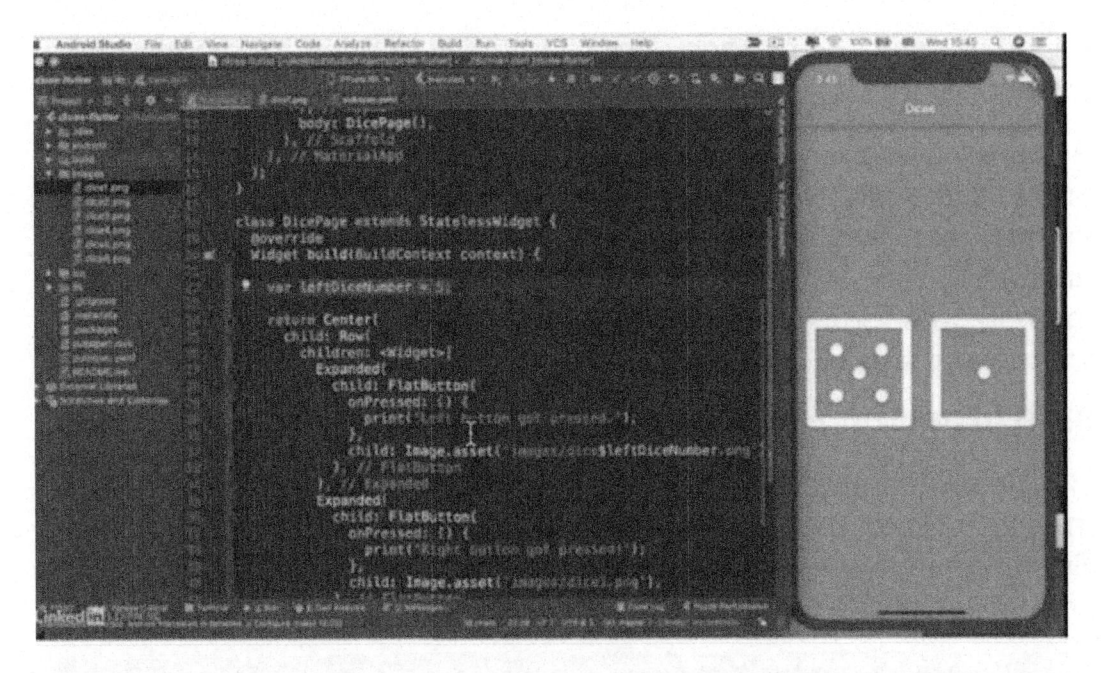

Now, instead of having this hard coded, just delete it and insert this variable. Just insert the dollar sign in your Dart terminal. Then, add one variable in front of the dollar sign. This will be the left dice number.

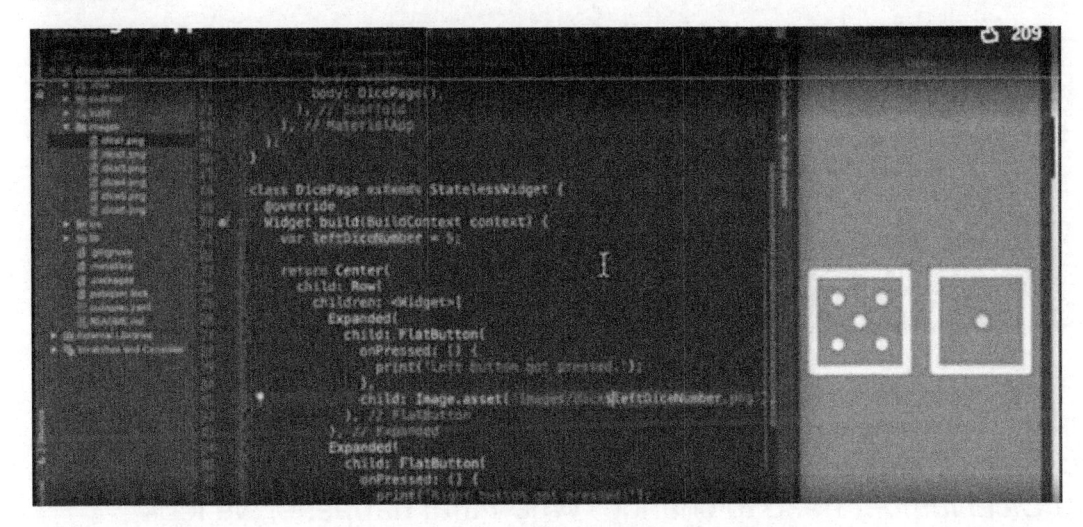

When we run the app again, you'll notice there's just one problem. If you change this variable to say five, and go ahead and click on hot reload or save, the change doesn't actually happen here because of the hot reload.

So, every piece of code within the terminal will be activated again and any changes will show. However, if our dice number isn't inside our build method, the change won't be shown in our app. So, you have to cut this and paste it into here. Then, if you hit save, this build method gets rerun, our left dice number gets set to five and wherever it's used gets updated.

8.2 Randomizing the Dice and Challenge One

Having switched up our stateless widget into a stateful widget, all the parts of our screen will update when the user interacts with it. So, the parts that need to change their state are now inside something called *DicePageState*.

In this case, we have a button that responds when the user presses on it. Therefore, when the user presses the button, a signal is sent to the app that we want to modify its state. All locations that use the *leftDiceNumber* need to change. When that happens, we look through this widget tree and our app will mark all the widgets that use that updated value.

It will put our new image widget and draw it again with the latest dice image. There's yet another problem! We're still updating the number here manually. If you type four and save it, and then press the button, it will change to four. But the user cannot change our code. So how can we get this *leftDiceNumber* to automatically change to a new random number between one and six?

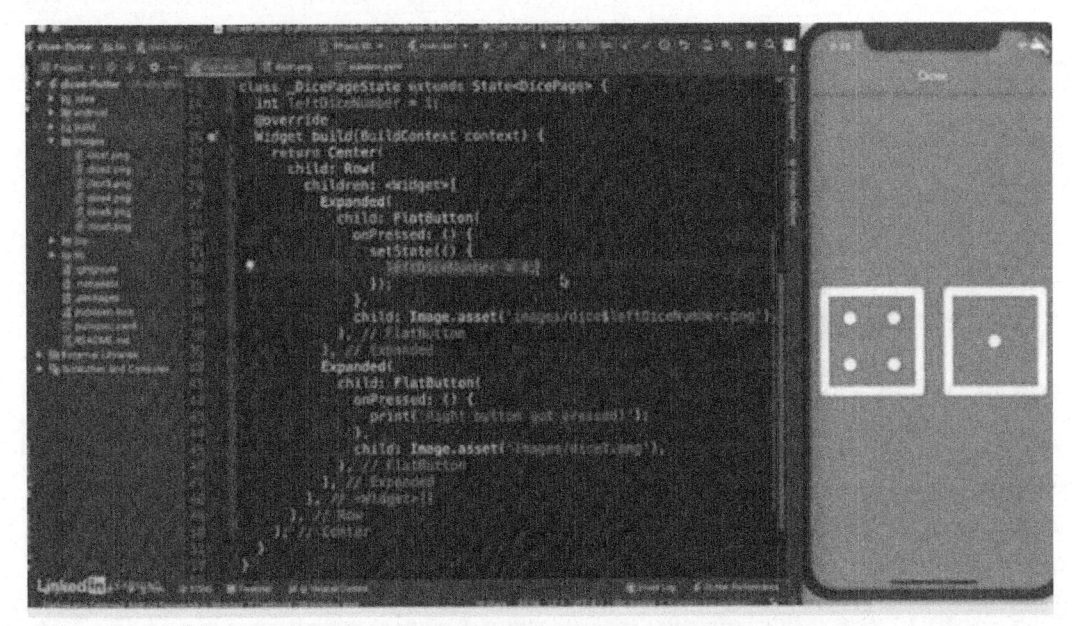

Well, we need to import a new library, the math library. In order to generate random numbers, we can check out the dart:math library. This is a library that contains all types of mathematical constants and functions, including a random number generator. Once you use this library in your code by importing it into your project, then your program will be able to generate random numbers. Let's go ahead and incorporate that into our project.

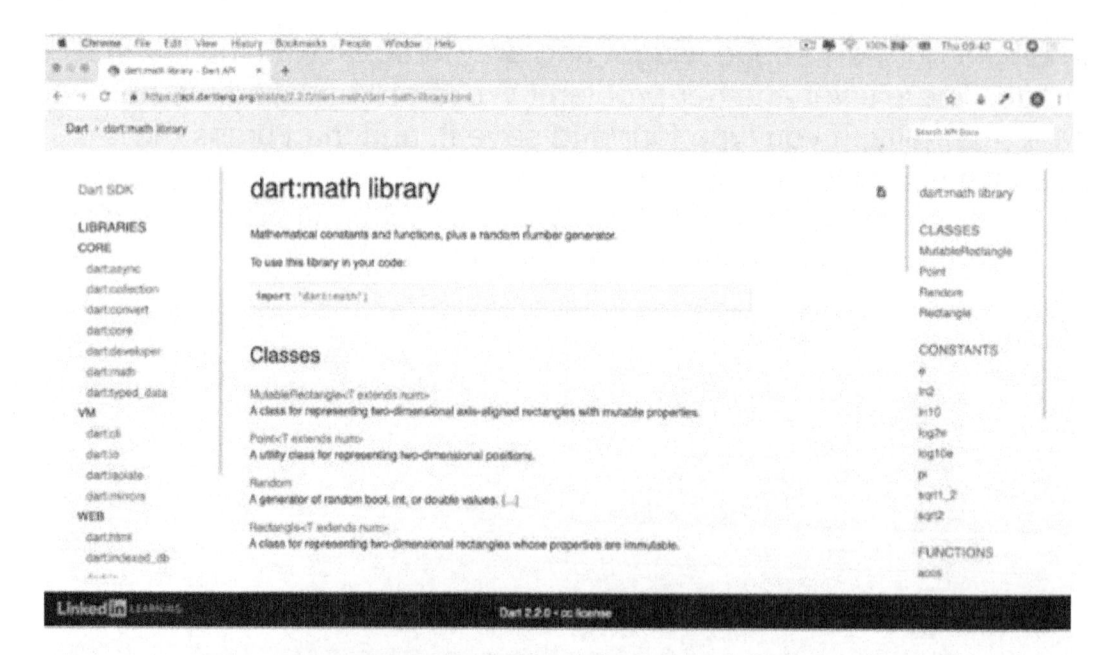

The material.dart library includes all the things we need, like how should a flat button look as opposed to a raised button. The fact that we're able to simply type out a widget like a flat button and it knows exactly what that should look like is because of the library. Start by writing "math", it'll find the right one for you. Hit Enter.

The math library will initially show up as gray, because it's telling you that you've imported this library, but you're not using it yet. Instead of setting our *leftDiceNumber* equal to four or three or one manually, which is quite painful, we'll use something that comes along with the math library, which is called *Random*. Random has a function called *nextInt*. Its function is to generate a non-negative random integer. So a random whole number from zero up to max, excluding the max.

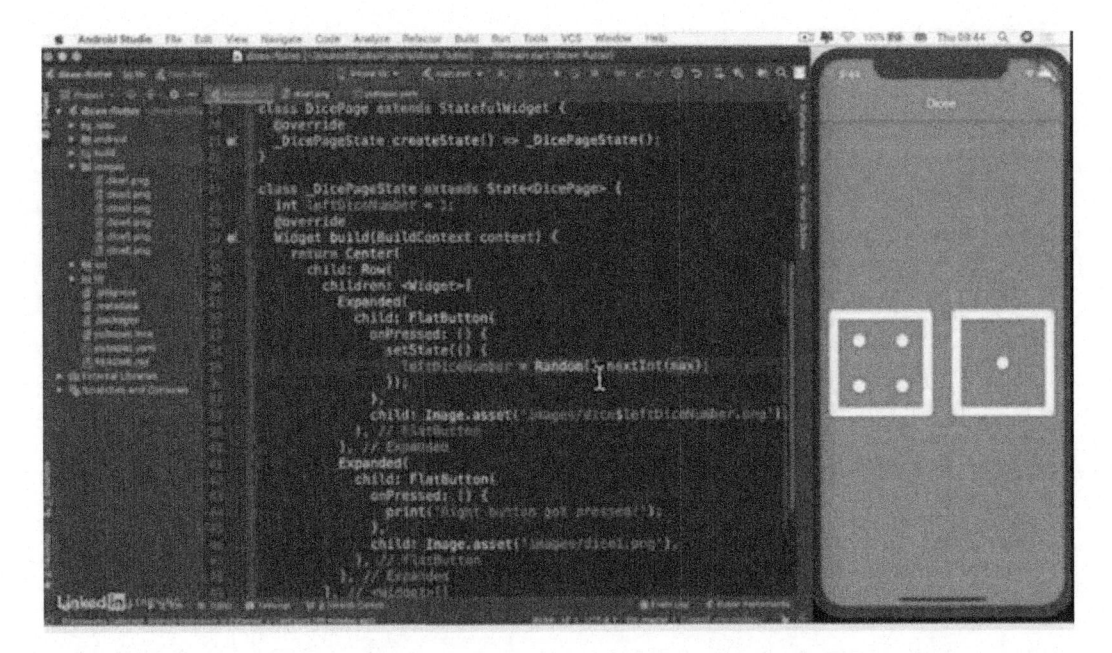

Max goes inside the parentheses of this *nextInt* function, and it will try to generate whole numbers from zero to whatever it is this number is, minus one. We're using the *Random* number generator that comes from our dart math library, and we're using a method called *nextInt* that comes from the Random number generator.

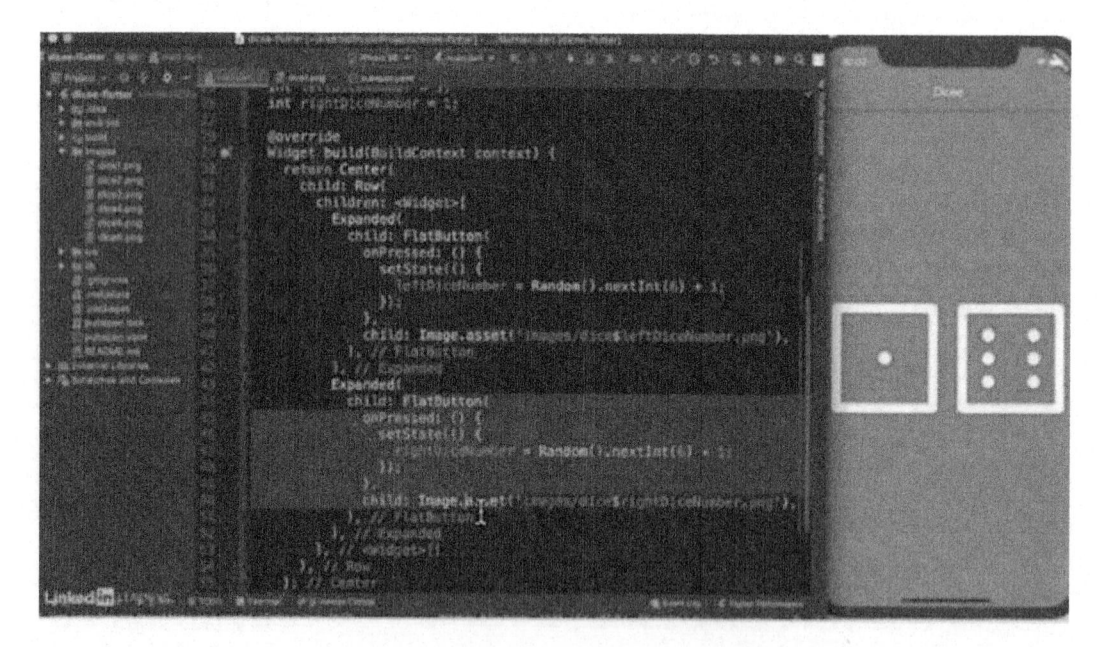

A maximum value is included between these parentheses. If we use six, what numbers do you think will be generated by our random number generator? Let's copy our line of code and head over to DartPad. Inside our main function, paste in our *leftDiceNumber* and add our *int* to create this new *leftDiceNumber*.

Import the dart math library so we can use our random number generator. We've created this new variable called *leftDiceNumber*. We'll set it to equal the random number generator using that *nextInt* method. So now all we have to do is just to print out our *leftDiceNumber* into the console, and click Run many times just to see what it'll print out.

Did you get five, one, or three? If you do this repeatedly, you'll find out that you'll get numbers between zero to six minus one. We'll get all the numbers between zero and five, so it could be any of those numbers. In our case, we can't actually have zero, because we don't actually have an image called *diceZero*.

What can we do to change that range from zero to five to one to six? We'll simply add one to this. If it's going to be a zero, it turns into one. If it's going to be a five, it turns into six.

Lastly, let's move over to the next challenge to see how we can be able to do the same thing that we did for the left dice, but for the right dice.

8.3 Challenge One Solution and Challenge Two

This challenge should be quite simple, as we've previously covered it once for the left dice. However, it's essential that we know how it all connects together. This is the essence of this challenge.

We already have a variable that's monitoring the value for our left dice number as well as updating it, when the button is pressed, so that we can show a new image in that image widget.

To do the same for the right dice, we'll create a new variable. Then, we'll just call it the right dice number. Now that we've got our variable, let's proceed to changing it to a random number, when the flat button is pressed.

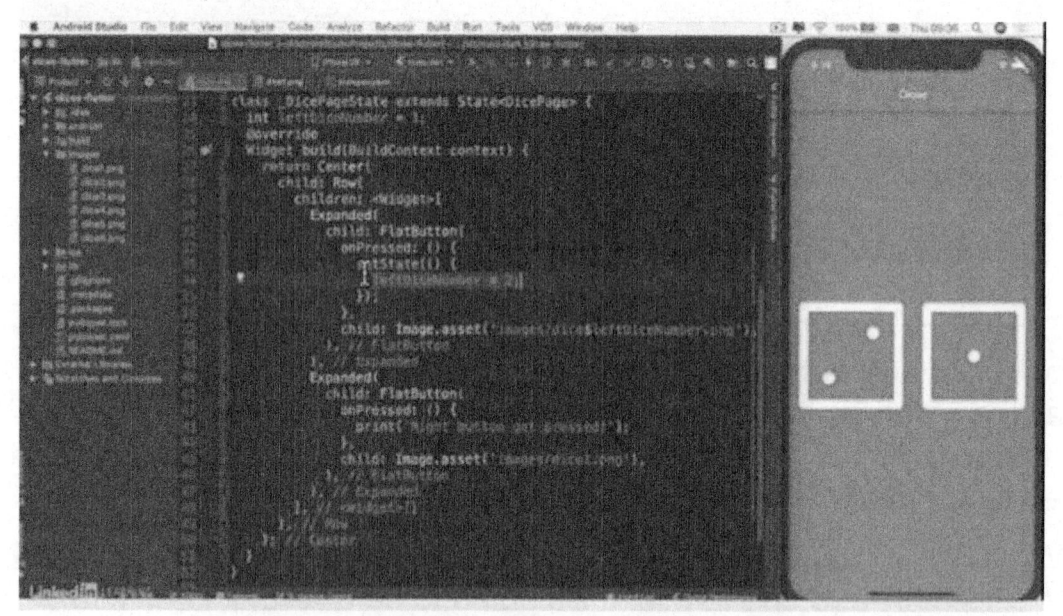

Inside the onPressed, the first thing is to affirm that the right dice number is going to be equal to a number that's generated from a random number generator. The specific number we will generate is an integer, which is a whole number.

Also, we're going to set the max to six, so that we generate random numbers between zero and five. Then, we'll add one to any of those numbers generated to bring it up to 'one to six'. This matches with the dice numbers that we have in our images.

We'll now update the place where we use that right dice number. So, instead of pulling up the **images/dice1.png**, which is pretty much hard-coded, it's always going to be the first image shown and we'll delete that one. Just use a string interpolation to insert the right dice number inside there, by using that little dollar sign there, that we saw previously in section 6.6.

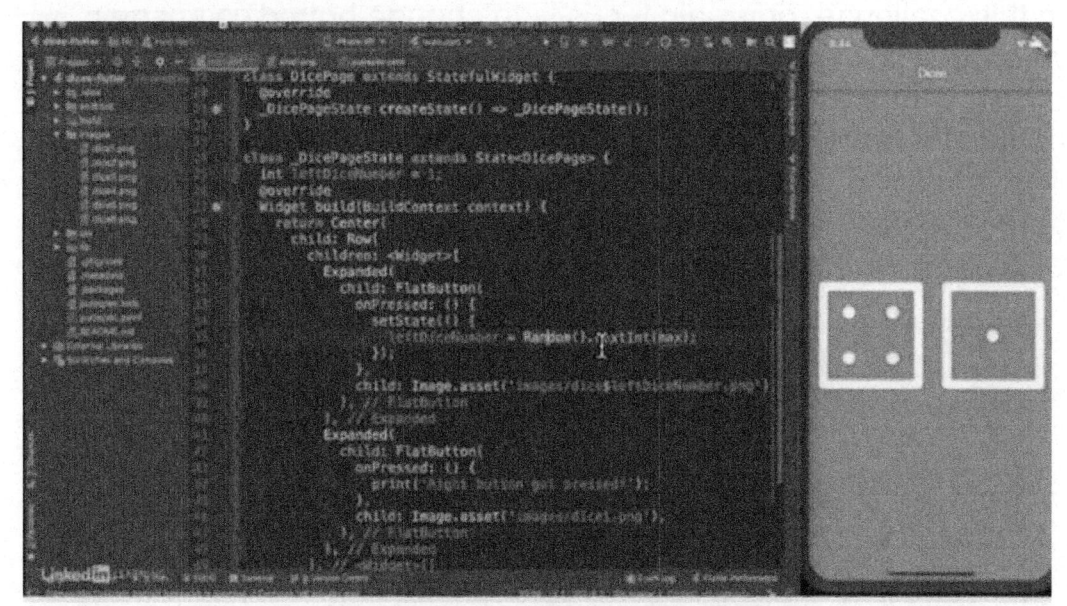

Having done that, when the right dice number changes, all the places where it's used will be updated. To do that, we have to call that method, *setState*. Simply, this means that this change in the right dice number's value, is going to trigger a rebuild of our state four widget, so that the parts where it's used can update on the screen.

Let's hit save for those changes to go through to our app . We already know the left side works and if we click on the right side, it also works. This gives us all the numbers that we could possibly need. So, we now have two separate dice, that we can roll on our dice app.

But, what if we wanted both dice to change, when one of the buttons is pressed? Or better still, what if we wanted both of these buttons to update when we click on any one of those buttons? Here is your challenge, try and get this behavior in your app.

8.4 Challenge Two Solution And Challenge Three

In this challenge, our main focus is to change both dice images when we click on any one of the buttons. We'll configure the app in such a way that both the *rightDiceNumber* and *leftDiceNumber* update themselves when we click on any one of these *FlatButtons*. The solution is quite simple. We need to generate a new number for both *leftDiceNumber* and *rightDiceNumber* whenever any of these buttons are pressed.

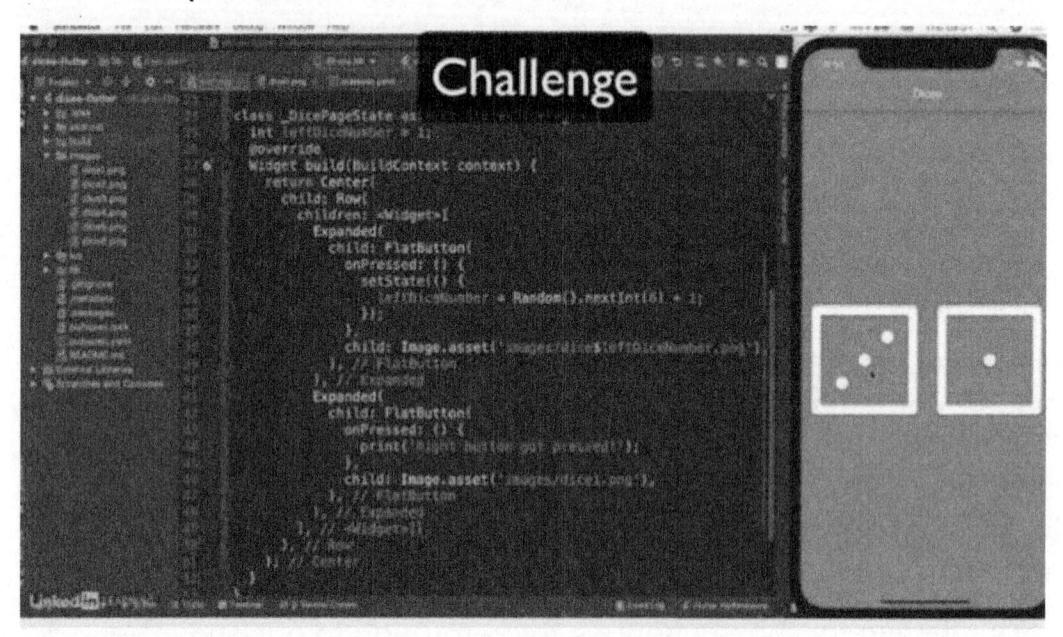

We'll simply copy the behavior that we have for the *rightDiceNumber* over here and also copy that line of code for the *leftDiceNumber* down here. Thus, whenever any one of the buttons are pressed, the *leftDiceNumber* is updated to a new random number. We update the *rightDiceNumber* into a new random number and call *setState* on that to update the *Image* on both of these places.

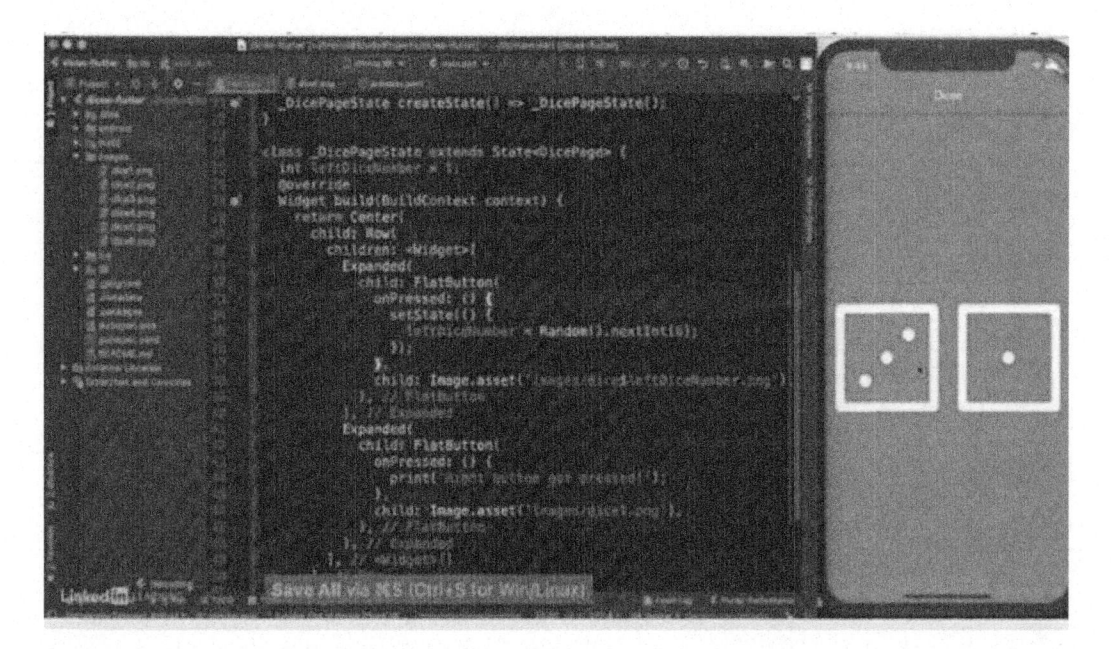

Now, *setState* sees that *leftDiceNumber* is used here as well as the *rightDiceNumber* when it is called. Thus, it will redraw both of these images. So, let's do it and hit Save. When I click on the left side, the right side changes. When I click on the right side, the left side also changes. Perfect, that's exactly what we wanted.

8.5 Challenge Three Solution

The simplest type of dart functions consists of a keyword, void at the beginning, the name of the function, a set of parentheses which we'll keep empty, and our curly braces. These curly braces contain all the instructions that are repeated and we need to use in different places in our code. Anytime we want to call this function or activate it, we call it by its name.

```
void getMilk ( ) {   //doSomething }
```

```
getMilk();
```

Applying the above concept to our code, let's create a new function. We'll start off with the void keyword. Let's call it *changeDiceFace* and add a set of empty parentheses. To complete building our function, we have to add a set of curly braces. We'll now add the blocks of code which are repeated across our code, namely updating our *leftDiceNumber* and *rightDiceNumber* within these curly braces. You can see that they're the same. Just cut that out of the *onPressed* and paste it into our new function.

Instead of having to write all those lines of code, simply call the method by name, which is *changeDiceFace*. Therefore, when our *FlatButton* is pressed, the *onPressed* listener is triggered. It will search to locate this function with a name of *changeDiceFace*. It finds it right here and it calls *setState*, changes the *leftDiceNumber* and *rightDiceNumber*. We can put that in here as well and call *changeDiceFace* down here too.

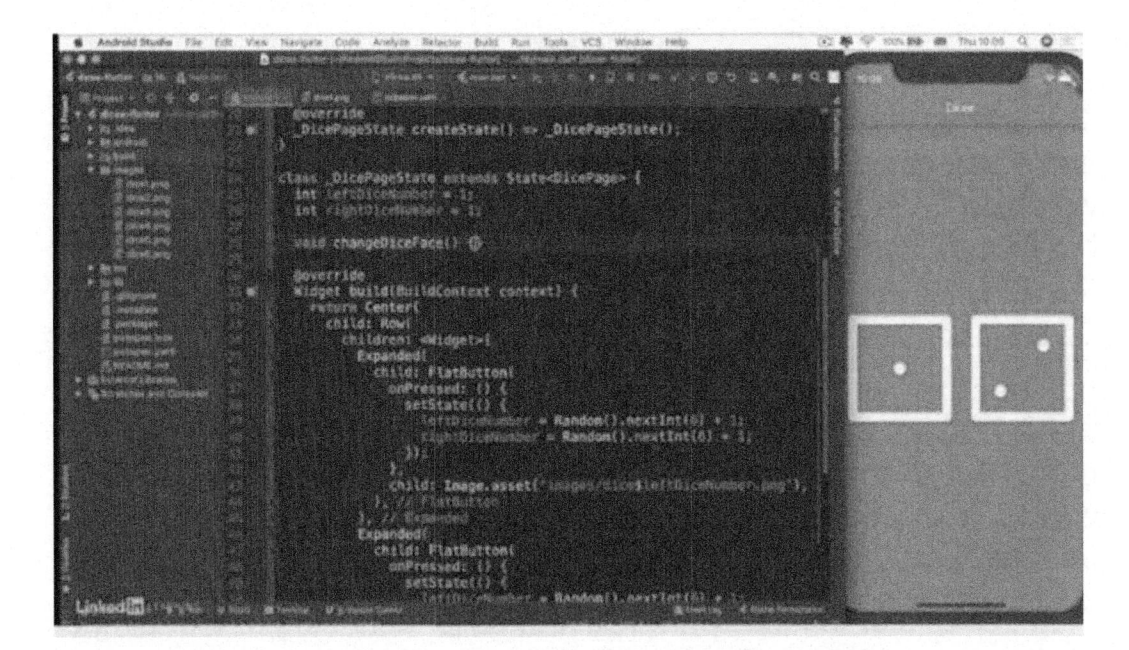

You can see now that this code is no longer repeated in two places. Or maybe if you had more dice, there would be more places that would be needed.

Chapter 8 Tip - Getting Familiar Is the Key

The challenges in this chapter are shown using a real-world project —a dice game app—that you can create and include in your Flutter portfolio. You can even start your new game app and build it, all by yourself. By so doing, you'll become very familiar with coding.

Final Words

The tech world is evolving at great speed as old technologies fall and new ones rise to the limelight all the time. If you've been watching and observing the mobile development scene, you'd likely have come across this new technology called Flutter.

Currently, Flutter is the top 12 software repos based on GitHub stars. Moreover, there are already numerous Flutter apps being published on app stores. This book cannot end without mentioning that the Xianyu app created by Alibaba team is one of the most prominent examples of apps created with Flutter that is still making waves. It is used by over 50 million people and more than 10 million people use it daily.

Flutter is one of the most innovative mobile technologies trending on the market right now. The benefits it brings to programmers and development teams make it a promising tool as the mobile technology of choice in the near future.

In this book, we found out that the central focus of Flutter revolves around widgets. The entire user interface (UI) is made of combining different widgets. Each of these widgets defines a structural element, such as a button or menu, a stylistic element like a font or color scheme, as well as an aspect of layout including padding and many more. Flutter offers custom widgets which look native either to Material Design for Android operating system or Cupertino for iOS apps. Hence, it does not use OEM widgets, but is capable of creating custom widgets.

As described in chapter one, one of the major benefits of using Flutter lies in its cross-platform functionality. It helps developers write one codebase for many apps including Android, iOS, and web. Mostly, Flutter depends on widgets and user interface (UI) designs. So, it only needs to compile and convert into an operating system

(OS) supported code, thereby helping developers to reduce their development time drastically.

More so, it has been projected by some experts that cross-platform development will attain its height in the years ahead and that Flutter will be the future of mobile app development. Whether you accept the fact that Flutter has come to stay or not is a personal choice. The fact remains that Flutter has penetrated almost all the spheres of the cross-platform app development space and it's not going away anytime soon.

Chapter two took us through the series of steps required for the installation of Flutter on your machine. Although the steps were simple and straightforward, there might be some hurdles to overcome during the installation process. This chapter took adequate care of them all in the troubleshooting section.

This book will not be complete without you performing the basic assignment: creating your first Flutter app from scratch. I know you enjoyed the task and every bit of information contained in this chapter.

In chapter five, we saw how Flutter offers fast compilation, which allows the development team to see the outcome of their code changes almost immediately, within a few milliseconds. This feature is called Hot Reload. This is one of the benefits that attracts developers to use Flutter as it allows them to make fast UI changes which translates to more productive mobile app development.

The importance of stateful and stateless widgets cannot be over-emphasized in Flutter app development. With them, building apps with state becomes easier. Chapter six dealt with various challenges including the dice app project, how to use expanded widgets for flexible layouts, intention actions, user interaction with Flutter buttons, and more.

You can do your best to create a state management library that will remain and completely align with the rest of the Flutter framework in its beauty and simplicity. As someone who is fascinated by UIs, using Flutter to create them will be a dream come true!

Flutter is really in high demand in the market ever since Google introduced the first stable release. Looking at the characteristics of Flutter, many questions might arise in your mind. Will corporations and businesses opt for Flutter as the number choice of developing apps? Is it the start of the end of developing native Android apps? Will Dart replace Java and Kotlin? Should native Android developers start learning Dart?

In as much as we will make no predictions concerning your choices, but the increased usage of Flutter could be the warning signal for native mobile app developers that Flutter might affect their role in the not so distant future.

If you've read through this book, you now have more reasons to start developing a Flutter app of your choice. The increased momentum displayed by Flutter over the past years and its continued adoption in enterprise apps, including consumer apps, shows that this is the way forward for app development.

Although Flutter requires you to be familiar with Dart, its syntax is simple and majority of the developers who are acquainted with JavaScript will find it quite easy to adopt. If you compare Flutter to React Native, Facebook's cross-platform framework, you'll discover that Flutter is good for UIs based widget sets. Besides, it provides excellent documentation and toolkits. Furthermore, Flutter is stable and can boast a growing number of developers and businesses that adopted it.

If this is exciting to you, get involved with more Flutter development projects today. Who knows, you might just turn into a Flutter coding pro!

Printed in Great Britain
by Amazon